CONTENTS

ACKNOWLEDGEMENTS

The project team would like to thank all the LEAs, schools and staff who participated in the project and gave up their time to complete the questionnaires and to be involved in the case study interviews.

We would also like to thank the advisory body (see Appendix A.1) and our NFER colleagues who participated in this project at various stages of the process: Jayne Osgood, Joanne Duff, Effie Sudell, Sam Addae, Mary Hargreaves and Joanna Le Métais.

EXECUTIVE SUMMARY

Context

In the Government's thrust to raise standards in education, the continuing professional development (CPD) needs of teachers, and the ways in which training and other activities might best be delivered, have received a high profile. The Government's CPD strategy (DfEE, 2001b) proposes a number of initiatives which aim to provide teachers with more opportunities for, access to and ownership of their own professional development. The strategy also puts forward a partnership approach to implementation, working with LEAs, schools, teachers, and other relevant organisations.

Aims and objectives

This study was carried out as part of the Local Government Educational Research Programme. It set out to investigate the current and potential role of the LEA in supporting schools to provide professional development for their staff, as part of their efforts to raise achievement. The project examined this at three levels: the LEA, the school and the teacher. The report captures the current practices and processes of CPD as experienced by teachers throughout England and Wales, and highlights the role of the LEA where appropriate.

The broad aims of the investigation were:

♦ to identify strategies in use in schools and LEAs to support the professional development of classroom teachers

♦ to provide detailed examples of innovative practice that might usefully be adopted by schools and LEAs wishing to make further improvements in their current provision.

Methodology

The research took place between April 2000 and July 2001, and comprised the following stages:

♦ a review of the strategies outlined in the available literature

♦ exploratory visits and telephone discussions with LEA and school staff

♦ a questionnaire survey, completed by 105 LEAs throughout England and Wales, asking for information on approaches to professional development and the nomination of schools with effective and/or innovative practice

♦ selection of 12 LEAs with different characteristics (size, geographical location, etc.) and different approaches to support for a questionnaire survey sent to 62 selected primary, secondary and special schools. This was completed by the headteacher or CPD coordinator from 42 schools

♦ case studies in 18 selected primary, secondary and special schools within seven LEAs. Altogether, 81 staff with varying roles and responsibilities were interviewed.

Main findings

Findings were examined at three levels: LEA, school and teacher, utilising data generated from the LEA questionnaire, school questionnaire and case study interviews with staff. The main findings are summarised below.

At the LEA level, the research highlights the significant role of the LEA in supporting teachers' CPD activities via: providing and facilitating CPD, the role of the adviser, encouraging and facilitating networks and support groups, and supplying information about CPD opportunities both within the LEA and further afield. It was found that the LEA should not only provide CPD that meets national priorities but should also use schools' School Development Plans (SDPs) to inform their Educational Development Plan (EDP), in the same way as schools predominantly use their SDPs to prioritise and direct their training needs. Furthermore, LEA-provided CPD was perceived as most appropriate when it met the needs of the school. This was most likely when the LEA staff were in touch with, and receptive to, the school's needs and context and when there was coordination between the LEA advisory team and the CPD coordinator/headteacher.

At the school level, headteachers were committed to developing opportunities for CPD. In many schools there was an expectation that teachers participated in CPD, and activities were more effective when there was a supportive ethos and culture of professional development in the school. Furthermore, the headteacher and/or the CPD coordinator played a fundamental role in teachers' CPD. They were identified as the gatekeepers to staff's participation in external CPD activities, receiving external CPD information; suggesting/recommending CPD to staff; and ultimately governing whether staff could participate in CPD. It was their role to bridge the gap between individual and SDP needs. In addition, they monitored staff feedback via formal/informal dissemination and evaluation forms. However, long-term monitoring and evaluation processes did not appear to be established. It would be appropriate for the LEA adviser to feed into this evaluation process, to evaluate the effectiveness of CPD and its impact in school. This process would also facilitate the provision of the most appropriate CPD.

At the individual level, CPD was seen as most effective when teachers were able to choose and direct their own professional development. Tensions sometimes existed between personal professional development requirements and schools' demands. Often teachers were participating in CPD to meet national priorities and to meet SDP requirements, sometimes at the expense of having a choice about developing their own particular interests and expertise.

The research found that effective CPD requires challenging and up-to-date content and must be relevant to classroom practice. The deliverer must have appropriate expertise and background knowledge. It was also important that clear, detailed and accurate information was provided to schools so that informed choices could be made.

It was the view that effective CPD should impact upon teaching and learning. However, it was not always easy for teachers to supply tangible evidence of impact. The biggest impact on teachers was their increased confidence, whilst the impact upon children's learning was said to be reflected in improved achievement levels, increased self-esteem and greater collaboration. There is clearly a need for LEAs and schools to develop systems for evaluating the short- and long-term impact of CPD activities in order to ensure that they make a significant contribution to raising standards of teaching and learning.

1. INTRODUCTION

The Government has demonstrated commitment to giving teachers training and support for their professional development. There is no doubt that continuing professional development (CPD) has a high profile, and there are initiatives in place to promote CPD for teachers. During the lifetime of the project, the General Teaching Council (GTC) was formed and the Government's CPD strategy has been launched (DfEE, 2001b).

This research study formed part of the Local Government Association (LGA) Educational Research Programme, and began in April 2000. Its intention was to identify strategies in place in schools and local education authorities (LEA) to support the professional development of classroom teachers.

The report provides a description of teachers' perception and experiences of CPD across England and Wales. It is based on a survey of LEAs and schools. A sample of schools was selected to provide greater insight into teachers' professional development and the role of the LEA. Illustrative examples are drawn from case study schools.

2. ABOUT THE PROJECT

2.1 Context

In the Government's thrust to raise standards in education, increasing attention is being paid to the continuing professional development (CPD) needs of teachers and to ways in which training and other activities might best be delivered. Recent developments in the education service in England and Wales have placed increased pressure on schools and teachers to bring about changes in classroom practices that will lead to improvements in the quality of teaching and learning. These have included the introduction of national policies such as OFSTED's inspection of teachers, the National Literacy and Numeracy Strategies, the publication of performance tables and the emphasis on target setting and raising standards, all of which have influenced the focus of professional development. More specifically, National Professional Qualifications for Headteachers (NPQH) training for headteachers and other strategies outlined in the Government's White and Green Papers have been aimed at CPD. Although there has been a strong focus on monitoring and evaluating the quality of teaching with these initiatives, relatively little has concentrated on the support mechanisms and the CPD activities needed to effect changes in teaching practices.

The Green Paper (DfEE, 1998) states that the Government is 'committed to giving teachers the training and support they need to do their jobs well and to progress in their careers'. Much of the chapter on training reinforces this approach: that teachers will have a contractual obligation to update their skills and knowledge on a regular basis; that they will be given opportunities to extend and develop their expertise and be given recognition for doing so. The Paper indicated that training and development activities would be provided within a framework that took account of three elements:

♦ national training priorities

♦ school priorities

♦ individual development needs.

It outlined that the Government would determine the focus of the national priorities; school priorities would emerge from school development planning; and individual needs would be identified through annual appraisal.

More recently, the Government published the Green Paper *Schools: Building on Success* (DfEE, 2001c) as the new framework for raising standards for all. As part of this broad framework, the Department for Education and Employment (now Department for Education and Skills) launched its strategy for teachers' continuing professional development 'Learning and

Teaching' on 1 March 2001. This was devised in consultation with the General Teaching Council (GTC), which has a specific remit to promote teachers' professional development, as well as the teacher unions and other organisations.

The strategy states that good professional development enables teachers to build upon their skills and keep up to date with the changing demands that are placed upon them. It also recognises that a professional development culture within schools creates a more supportive and encouraging environment. The strategy aims to provide more opportunities for teachers to share good practice through professional development in other schools, and to learn from colleagues' expertise and experience. There is also an emphasis upon teachers taking responsibility for their own professional development, and funds will be provided so that teachers can choose and direct their own professional development. In the light of this, the OFSTED inspection framework will be revised to include a section on the professional development of staff and the arrangements that the school makes to identify and address these needs.

As part of the strategy, there will be:

- a CPD website, providing teachers with up-to-date information. It will also include case studies of good practice, course information, opportunities to network, etc.

- a Code of Practice entitled 'Good Value CPD' (DfEE, 2001a) which sets out what schools and teachers can expect from providers of CPD, such as LEAs and higher education institutions (HEIs)

- the appointment of more Advanced Skills teachers

- encouragement of good practice sharing via Beacon Schools

- opportunities for teachers to open an Individual Learning Account

- encouragement of schools to seek Investors in People recognition.

An extra £92 million funding will be forthcoming over the next three years. It will aim to:

- provide new opportunities: sabbaticals and an early professional development scheme

- extend existing programmes: Best Practice research scholarships, professional bursaries, and teachers' international professional development.

The Government's focus on raising standards of teaching and learning via the CPD strategy aims to take a partnership approach in its implementation with LEAs, schools, teachers and other relevant organisations. The National Foundation for Education Research (NFER) project is, therefore, timely in examining the current and future role of the LEA in supporting teachers' continuing professional development.

2.2 Background and aims

The project was set up as part of the LGA Educational Research Programme and was carried out by NFER. The investigation had two main aims:

♦ to identify strategies in use in schools and LEAs to support the professional development of classroom teachers

♦ to provide detailed examples of innovative practice that might usefully be adopted by schools and LEAs wishing to make further improvements in their current provision.

The research investigated the current and potential role of the LEA in supporting schools to provide professional development for their staff, as part of their efforts to raise achievement. It explored the process by which LEAs work with schools to set whole-school targets, to identify the training and development needs arising, and to provide appropriate in-service training and advisory support, which meets the needs of the schools, individual teachers and classroom assistants.

The project examined a range of the strategies that schools used to improve the quality of teaching, such as external and in-school training courses, mentoring systems, classroom observations with feedback, video analyses and action research. Perceptions of the effectiveness of the main strategies identified will be described and analysed.

2.3 Methodology

2.3.1 Research design

The research involved:

• a review of the strategies outlined in the available literature

• exploratory visits and telephone discussions with LEA and school staff

• a questionnaire survey of LEAs, asking for information on approaches to professional development and the nomination of schools with effective and/or innovative practice

• the selection of 12 LEAs with different characteristics (size, location, etc.) and different approaches to support

• a questionnaire survey of nominated schools in the case study LEAs

• case studies in selected schools within seven LEAs.

The review of the literature was ongoing. Strategies for supporting CPD were identified from the review and used to inform exploratory visits and telephone discussions with LEA and school staff and to generate the questions for the questionnaire.

2.3.2 The LEA survey

A short questionnaire was sent to all LEAs in England and Wales, asking for information about their approaches to CPD and for the nomination of schools with interesting and innovative practice. LEA personnel were asked to provide information about:

- the methods used to identify the CPD needs of teachers in each LEA
- the CPD activities on offer to teachers in each authority
- the providers of the activities
- the ways in which CPD activities were evaluated and monitored.

The questionnaire also provided an opportunity for LEAs to nominate a maximum of six schools, in which they felt examples could be found of effective or innovative practice in terms of the approach taken to providing CPD for teachers. The nominations provided information to enable selection of schools for in-depth case studies, planned for phase two of the research.

Survey administration

NFER link officers in all 175 LEAS in England and Wales were sent a copy of the questionnaire, along with a prepaid envelope for returns, in June 2000. A letter outlining the aims and methodology of the research project was enclosed and the confidential nature of the survey outlined, in order to maximise the quantity and quality of returns and to encourage LEAs to provide detailed responses. The officers were asked either to complete the questionnaire themselves, or to pass it on to an officer with direct responsibility for CPD.

Timescale

The summer term is a notoriously difficult time to generate good response rates to surveys; therefore a strategy was employed for chasing late returns. The cut-off date had been set for 30 June, so telephone enquiries were made during the last week of June and questionnaires were subsequently reissued by either post, fax or e-mail. This approach generated a greater response than would normally have been expected, although a small number were returned after the deadline date.

Response rate

Of the 175 LEAs in England and Wales contacted, 105 returned completed questionnaires by the deadline; hence an overall response rate of 60 per cent was achieved. Not only were all types of authority represented in the returned questionnaire, but there was also diversity in terms of geographical location and size (see Table 2.1).

Table 2.1 Response rate

	Sample		Population	
Type of LEA	**Number**	**% of total sample**	**Number**	**% of total population**
Inner London Boroughs	3	3	13	7
Outer London Boroughs	11	10	20	11
Metropolitan Boroughs	20	19	37	21
Welsh	15	14	22	13
Unitary Authorities	30	29	47	27
Counties	26	25	36	21
Total	**105**	**100**	**175**	**100**

All responses to the open-ended questions were coded in order that quantitative analysis could be carried out. The analysis involved calculating frequencies of particular responses to individual items. These frequencies were analysed by the type of LEA as outlined above, but differences between the types of LEA were not particularly illuminating, so most of the results reported do not distinguish between types of LEA but present a more general national picture.

School nominations

LEAs were asked to nominate up to six schools in the authority. For a variety of reasons, not all LEAs in the sample felt able to nominate schools. Some questionnaires had been completed by people new to the post who did not have access to appropriate information, and others were reluctant to suggest schools in the *'interest of reducing the bureaucratic burden'*. However, 81 LEAs nominated between two and six schools, although the majority nominated six. A total of 436 schools were nominated (see Table 2.2).

Table 2.2 School nominations

Type of school	**Number nominated**
Nursery	4
Primary	206
Middle	10
Secondary	139
6th Form	10
Special	19

Further analysis was carried out on the information on schools, provided by the LEAs, to identify the range of innovative and effective CPD activities currently in place.

Innovative and effective CPD

Many respondents gave in-depth details about the CPD activities operating in each nominated school, but other LEAs offered '*good CPD*' without more explicit clarification. From the analysis, the patterns outlined in Table 2.3 emerged.

Table 2.3   Innovative and effective examples of CPD activities

Reason for nominating	Frequency of responses
In-school CPD	212
External CPD	147
Clear leadership	56
Whole school	34
Well-established CPD	33
Locally based	30
Part of a national strategy	11
Recovering school	13
Curriculum-focused	9
Hidden curriculum	7

81 of the 105 LEAs in the sample responded to this part of the survey. Respondents could give more than one response.

The information was used to select schools for the school survey and influenced the selection of schools for the case studies.

2.3.3 The school survey

Twelve LEAs, representing a range of size, type and geographical location, were selected. Nominated schools included secondary, primary and special. A short questionnaire, focusing on professional development activities and processes, was sent to headteachers of nominated schools. The questionnaire asked for information on:

* processes for identifying teachers' CPD needs

* available activities

* providers

* evaluation

* monitoring

* effectiveness

* examples of practice in their school.

Survey administration

Questionnaires were sent to a total of 62 primary, secondary and special schools in 12 LEAs in England and Wales in September 2000. A letter outlining the aims and methodology of the research project was enclosed and the confidential nature of the survey outlined. Headteachers were asked either to complete the questionnaire themselves or to pass it on to their CPD coordinator.

Timescale

Respondents were asked to reply within two weeks of receiving the questionnaire. A few schools were reminded by telephone soon after the deadline, in an attempt to increase the response rate.

Response rate

Forty-two questionnaires were completed and returned and a further four were returned after the deadline. The content of the late-returned questionnaires was not included in the statistical analysis but, where appropriate, contributed to the qualitative analysis.

A response rate of over 60 per cent was achieved. Table 2.4 shows the variety and range of LEAs and schools which completed the questionnaire.

Table 2.4   Schools in LEAs responding to the questionnaire

Response details	Primary	Secondary	Special
Inner London Borough	3	1	0
Outer London Borough	2	3	2
Metropolitan Borough	5	2	0
Welsh	7	0	0
Counties	4	1	1
New Authorities	5	5	1
Total	26	12	4

All responses to the open-ended questions were coded so that quantitative analysis could be carried out, although the small number of questionnaires limited the extent of the statistical analysis. Frequencies of particular responses to individual items were calculated. Attempts were not made to analyse responses according to LEA or school type, because the focus was to identify a range of activities, support strategies and any impact on teaching and learning.

2.3.4 Case study interviews

Respondents (to the returned school questionnaires) were asked to indicate whether they were willing to describe their practice in more detail and to continue their participation in the project as case study schools. Most respondents agreed. This enabled schools to be selected to represent different school types and range of CPD provision. In total, 18 schools were selected across England and Wales. Table 2.5 reveals the composition of schools that took part in the case study interviews during Spring 2001.

Table 2.5   Composition of schools in case study interviews

LEAs	Primary	Secondary	Special
7	12	3	3

As can be seen, the schools were from seven LEAs across England and Wales. The types of LEAs involved were: Wales, Metropolitan, Unitary, County, Outer London. There were more primary schools in the case study sample, as primary schools were nominated more frequently than secondary or special schools by LEA respondents and more of them agreed to share their practice with NFER researchers.

Staff of varying roles and responsibilities took part in the interviews. The researchers asked to interview the headteacher, CPD coordinator and several other staff who had been involved in CPD activities, within each school. In total, 81 staff were interviewed: Appendices A2.1, A2.2 and A2.3 reveal the range of interviewees and the responsibilities which they held by school type (primary, secondary, special).

The roles and responsibilities were specified by staff at the time of interview. In most cases, all interviewees (except all headteachers) had teaching commitments as well as their specified roles. Furthermore, staff who indicated that they were subject coordinators may have been a coordinator for more than one subject within their school (this is not specified in the tables). The interviewees also represented staff at different stages of their teaching/school career, ranging from two years up to 35 years. Thus, insight into the CPD experiences was drawn from a wide range of staff across the spectrum, in terms of their school responsibilities, age and length of teaching/school experience.

Most interviews were conducted individually with staff members; except, in a few cases, where joint interviews were carried out by request. The researcher initially explained the background to the project and that staff's responses would be confidential; no school nor individual would be named in the research. The interview schedule comprised open-ended questions which aimed to capture staff's views and experiences of CPD in their school and within their LEA. There were schedules devised for the headteacher/CPD coordinator, and for other teaching staff. The questions asked all interviewees to talk about the following:

- their views of CPD

- their own CPD experiences

- processes of involvement

- conditions for effective CPD

- support strategies in the school

- support strategies in the LEA

- impact upon teaching and learning
- effective CPD
- future CPD.

Staff could report their CPD experiences in general, or in relation to a specific activity in which they had been involved. The interviews lasted approximately 45 minutes; individuals and schools were thanked for the time they had given up to be involved in the research. In addition, interviews were conducted with three LEA advisers, to ascertain their views and experiences of CPD activities within their area. The advisers were selected because they were available on the day that the researcher visited their area, and their responses were used to expand upon the findings elicited from the LEA questionnaire.

2.4 Report structure

This report takes a thematic approach to examining the current and future role of the LEA in supporting teachers' continuing professional development, capturing the current practices and processes that constitute CPD as reported by teachers within schools. Each section is approached from three levels: the LEA, school and teacher levels, using data from both the questionnaires (LEA and school) and the case study interviews with the LEA advisers and school staff. The report chapters address the following themes:

- definition of CPD
- types of CPD activities that teachers are involved in
- processes of need identification, involvement and evaluation of CPD activities
- conditions for effective CPD
- support strategies within school
- support strategies from the LEA
- impact on teaching and learning
- future CPD activities.

At the end of each chapter, there is a summary of the main findings and, where appropriate, implications for the role of the LEA are highlighted.

3. DEFINING CPD

In the Teacher Training Agency/Market and Opinion Research International (MORI, 1995) survey of CPD, over 4,000 respondents (teachers, INSET coordinators and INSET providers) defined CPD as 'activities whose main purpose was the development of teachers' professional knowledge, understanding and skills so as to improve the quality of teaching and learning in the classroom'. This description clearly focuses upon the impact that CPD will have upon teaching and learning. However, the DfEE strategy for teachers' CPD (DfEE, 2001b) reported that 'for many teachers, their image of CPD is still one-off events or short courses, often away from the school, of variable quality and relevance, delivered by a range of external providers'. This suggests that CPD is often recognised by teachers only in terms of external activities and that in-school CPD is often overlooked.

In the NFER study, in order to ascertain staff's understanding of CPD and as a start point to the case study interviews, staff were first asked what they thought constituted CPD. The researchers further elaborated by asking what kinds of activities they thought helped to develop teachers professionally.

Table 3.1 shows the number of staff within the three school types (primary, secondary and special) and their reported views of CPD. Four main themes were elicited from the interviews: staff talked about their own (or colleagues) CPD experiences, they gave examples of activities that they felt constituted CPD, they expressed their general attitude and outlook towards CPD, or they discussed challenges to undertaking professional development activities.

Table 3.1   Defining CPD, by staff within the three school types

Response categories	Frequency of response by staff		
	Primary N=42	Secondary N=15	Special N=16
Reports of their own CPD experiences	30	9	10
Examples of CPD activities	29	7	5
General attitude	15	6	6
Challenges to CPD	6	3	6

Most staff talked about their own CPD experiences or those of their colleagues, referring to activities that they were currently, or had recently been, involved in. A wide range of experiences was mentioned and these will be reported in detail in Chapter 4, where staff's responses to a series of questions about their own CPD experiences are discussed.

Staff also chose to talk about examples of CPD and the types of activities that they felt helped teachers develop professionally. All staff from the three school types mentioned a diverse range of activities, such as: meetings (staff, cluster), lesson observations, mentoring, discussions with colleagues, action research, INSET, workshops, LEA courses, diplomas, LEA adviser visits. As can be seen, both in-school and external activities were reported. These, of course, may have been CPD activities that staff had themselves experienced, or their responses may demonstrate a broader understanding of the types of opportunities that are available.

It was interesting that staff also chose to talk about their general attitude towards CPD; more headteachers than other staff members mentioned these global views. The main themes focused upon the approach, the process and the outcomes of CPD activities (each of these themes is discussed in more depth throughout the report). Firstly, it was reported that CPD should focus upon the development of the whole school: it is not just teachers who should be involved in professional development, but rather the whole school community including caretaker and administrative staff. The school ethos was viewed as central to providing professional development opportunities for all staff members and fostering an environment where staff were encouraged to develop.

> *Professional development is for everyone.* (Primary headteacher)

> *CPD is an important part of the school ethos and framework.*
> (Secondary headteacher)

Linked to this issue was whether CPD is about meeting the needs of the individual and/or the school.

> *CPD needs to be tailor-made for the school.*
> (Primary, CPD coordinator)

It was also reported that CPD is about staff becoming reflective practitioners, self-evaluating their practice, and widening their perspective. The impact of CPD upon teaching and learning also was often mentioned; CPD should improve teaching skills, practice and confidence.

> *CPD is where staff can develop their skills and subject knowledge.*
> (Primary headteacher)

> [CPD includes] *everything that engages teachers in becoming reflective practitioners.* (Primary headteacher)

The fourth category of responses, mentioned to a lesser extent by staff, referred to the challenges and barriers to undertaking CPD. These challenges were mainly focused around the following three themes:

◆ time constraints

◆ delivery of CPD (style, practicalities/arrangements, content)

◆ budget/resource limitations.

Comments about time constraints centred upon the lack of time within school to get colleagues together, and to undertake CPD. One staff member reported that she would have liked to take on extra studies, but she had a young family at home. Thus, there was an assumption that time and commitment outside school hours was required to undertake CPD activities. Staff also briefly talked about effective CPD, with regard to the delivery: style, content and practicalities/arrangements were mentioned. In particular, staff stated that lecture style delivery was not very useful, that the content needed to be appropriately targeted (e.g. towards special needs), and that the arrangement of CPD activity was critical (e.g. after-school hours, near to school). Staff also reported that budget limitations often restricted the choice of CPD activities.

Staff responses to this first question, on the interview schedule, provided an opening to the discussion of CPD. It was clear that staff preferred to talk about their own experiences of CPD activities. A wide range of issues was raised, and these were further discussed throughout the case study interviews. The following chapters will explore these issues in more depth.

4. CPD ACTIVITIES AVAILABLE FOR SCHOOL STAFF

The CPD Strategy (DfEE, 2001b) is designed to ensure that teachers are given more opportunities for relevant, focused, effective professional development.

This section describes the kinds of CPD activities identified in the NFER project as being available to school staff. The LEA survey data provided a broad picture and the school survey highlighted activities that schools were undertaking. The case study interviews provided more detail about some of the activities, and examples are included.

From the surveys and the case study interviews, it was clear that an extensive range and variety of CPD activities were available for school staff. The first part of this chapter considers the types of CPD activities available.

4.1 LEA and school responses

Questionnaires to LEAs and schools asked respondents about the kinds of CPD activities that were available to them. Their responses to predetermine options are presented in Table 4.1.

Some activities were provided by the LEA, others were facilitated by the LEA, but school responses did not distinguish.

4.1.1 Activities provided by the LEA

LEA respondents indicated that in-school training was the most frequent CPD activity that they provided for teachers. One-off conferences, seminars and workshops were the next most frequently cited activities. Other activities provided by the LEA included observation, in-class support and networking forums.

4.1.2 Activities facilitated by the LEA

LEA respondents identified their role in facilitating CPD activities and indicated that higher academic and higher professional accredited courses were the most common of these. One-off conferences were the third most frequently cited activity that LEAs facilitated.

Table 4.1   Representation of CPD activities available to teachers as identified by LEA and school respondents

Activity	Frequency of LEA responses				Frequency of school responses	
	Activities provided	*Order*	Activities facilitated	*Order*	Activities undertaken	*Order*
In-school training	104	*1*	45	*6*	91	*3*
One-off conferences	103	*2*	59	*3*	115	*1*
One-off seminars	98	*3*	49	*5*	80	*4*
One-off workshops	98	*4*	42	*8*	99	*2*
Observation of colleagues	93	*5*	23	*11*	73	*5*
In-class support	92	*6*	19	*13*	61	*6*
Networking forums	92	*7*	23	*11*	47	*10*
Ongoing non-accredited programmes	85	*8*	37	*10*	48	*9*
Mentoring of colleagues	77	*9*	41	*9*	56	*7*
Visiting other schools	63	*10*	43	*7*	52	*8*
Action research	45	*11*	55	*4*	42	*11*
Higher/professional accredited courses	32	*12*	71	*2*	37	*12*
Higher academic accredited courses	24	*13*	76	*1*	33	*13*
Other activities	10		8		5	
No response	0		3		0	
Total	1016		594		839	

Based on 105 LEAs and 42 schools.   Respondents could give more than one response.

Respondents in the school survey cited one-off conferences as the CPD activity that was most frequently available, followed by one-off workshops and in-school training.

Although the most common of the activities facilitated by LEAs, higher academic and professional accredited courses were cited least frequently by LEA and school respondents.

Alternative providers were identified by survey respondents as higher education institutions (HEIs), further education (FE) colleges, private consultants, and others (unspecified). Details are provided in Table 4.2

Table 4.2   Alternative providers identified by LEA respondents

Activity	Provider			
	HE	FE	Private consultants	Other
One-off conferences	38	3	47	27
One-off seminars	24	4	31	21
One-off workshops	21	6	37	23
Ongoing non-accredited programmes	32	3	11	13
In-school training	19	3	33	18
Action research	47	1	5	13
Higher academic programmes	77	3	3	1
Higher professional programme	58	3	7	12
Visits to other schools	2	0	6	22
Networking forums	6	1	11	15
In-class support	1	0	12	10
Monitoring colleagues	12	0	12	20
Observation	1	0	10	13
Total	338	27	232	198

Based on 105 LEAs. Respondents could give more than one response.

In the school survey, respondents identified providers for different activities as outlined in Table 4.3.

Table 4.3   Providers of CPD activities as indicated by school respondents

Activity	Provider					
	School	LEA	HEI	Private consultants	FE	Other
One-off conferences	24	38	14	26	5	8
One-off workshops	32	32	9	16	1	9
In-school training	40	23	8	18	2	0
One-off seminars	20	25	11	14	2	8
Observations of colleagues	42	24	2	4	1	0
In-class support	35	22	0	4	0	0
Mentoring colleagues	39	12	2	1	1	1
Visiting other schools	37	13	2	0	0	0
On going non-accredited programmes	11	18	8	3	6	2
Networking forum	12	23	3	3	2	4
Action research	17	9	11	0	3	2
Higher professional courses	4	9	14	1	5	4
Higher academic courses	4	3	19	0	6	1
Observation – unspecified	0	0	0	0	0	5
Total	317	251	103	90	34	44

Based on 42 schools. Respondents could give more than one response.

4.2 Types of CPD activities undertaken in the case study schools

As Table 4.3 shows, schools viewed themselves as significant providers and this was reflected in the case study schools. In most primary schools, the headteachers and the subject coordinators had a key role, while in other schools the deputy, the SENCO and individual teachers also led activities. Only two primary teachers said that they provided their own CPD in the form of reading educational journals or researching on the internet.

In secondary schools, the CPD coordinators and staff involved in Improving the Quality of Education for All (IQEA) (see Appendix 4.4) were deemed to provide CPD activities while special school staff were able to draw upon the headteacher and coordinators as well as a speech therapist, a nurse and a dietician.

The LEA was an important provider in the case study schools, and a variety of alternative providers were identified.

Interviewees varied in their length of service and number of years of post. Appendices A4.1, A4.2 and A4.3 show the staff involved in different types of activity. One respondent in the school survey suggested that CPD activities should match the needs and experience of the teacher. For example, the most effective approach for a newly qualified teacher (NQT) was a good mentor and discussion time. However, the case study interviews did not reveal a pattern of involvement in relation to teachers' length of service or number of years in post. Participation seemed to be linked to school requirements and, in some cases, individual teachers' needs (see Chapter 5).

To provide more detail about the CPD activities available, interviewees were asked about CPD activities in which they had been involved. They talked about those that were most recent and those that they viewed most positively.

Interviewees' responses fell into different categories. They identified in-school activities that were school focused and school based. For those activities, staff worked on issues identified by the school and they were undertaken within the school. Other activities were school focused but were carried out elsewhere. Some activities were concerned with individual teachers' professional development and were not always linked to the school focus. Another group of activities was where staff had a wider view and were involved with other schools within the LEA, e.g. cluster groups and feeder school groups.

Some activities identified were not frequently encountered in the schools visited but were identified by individual schools or teachers and contributed to professional development. Such activities included: using the internet, attending evening classes, making a video, organising after-school clubs, working with parent groups, exploring ideas for an MSc and reading.

4.2.1 CPD activities that occur when there are no children in school

The times that are available for CPD activities when there are no children in school are the closure days and after school or during staff meeting times.

Closure days

Many schools saw closure days as providing valuable opportunities for staff development (see also Harland *et al.*, 1999).

Closure days were particularly appreciated for developing teamwork and departmental expertise (see Table 4.4).

Table 4.4   CPD activities undertaken by teachers on closure days

Time provided	Types of activity		
	Primary	**Secondary**	**Special**
Closure days	• using the LEA adviser or private consultants to work with teachers • developing whole-school approaches • establishing working groups within the school • initiating a starting point for CPD • consolidating/ sharing activities • identifying the next steps for CPD	• developing team-work within a department • creating subject documentation/ policies • working with consultants • developing subject expertise • sharing good practice across the school (curriculum tour)	• meeting in teams • attending pyramid INSET • taking part in curriculum-based activities to take account of observations, children's needs and specialist areas

Based on three primary schools, three secondary schools and two special schools

Primary teachers were disappointed that so many of their closure days were used for Government or LEA initiatives rather than for school-identified needs. In one primary school, however, the whole school had used the closure day to evaluate a resource and to consolidate their team.

All three secondary schools mentioned CPD activities undertaken in the closure days. These were considered to be particularly useful when departments had the opportunity to work together on an issue that they had identified for their focus. In one school, a 'curriculum tour' had been organised.

The curriculum tour is interesting and worthwhile as it provides an opportunity to meet with other departments, to look at their resources and their approach. This is arranged like a market: each department has a stall whereby they present their resources and talk about their experience; it is useful to see what other subjects could adopt. (Secondary school teacher)

After-school meetings and staff meetings

In many schools, some staff meetings were given over to professional development while other meetings focused on management and business issues (see Table 4.5). In primary and secondary schools, after-school CPD sessions were held on a regular basis – sometimes for a whole-school focus and at other times for a departmental or subject focus. Some secondary interviewees found the departmental focus more relevant than the whole-school focus meetings.

Table 4.5   CPD activities undertaken after school/or during staff meetings

Time provided	Types of activity		
	Primary	**Secondary**	**Special**
After school/ staff meetings	• working groups • cascading information, leading INSET and reporting back on activities attended outside school • focusing on specific issues, e.g. target setting, literacy/ numeracy, SEN • undertaking tailor-made activities for the school • moderating and sharing coordinator skills	• delivering national initiatives, for example NOF training • developing Beacon status • talking and deciding in groups how an approach might be implemented	• meeting twice a week at the end of the school day • attending HEI-delivered Master's course modules

Based on seven primary schools, two secondary schools and two special schools

On closure days and after school, two kinds of CPD activities were identified: leading and attending staff discussion groups, and LEA advisers or consultants working with the teaching team.

Leading and attending staff discussion groups

It is worth noting that several primary school interviewees considered the process of leading the discussion group or reporting back to staff meetings to be part of their own professional development.

Examples included:

- being a facilitator for other staff in their own school or in another school

- undertaking mentor training and having an input to courses for NQTs

- working with parents

- replacing other curriculum coordinators who were unable to attend an activity.

In a special school, one of the team integrated children into mainstream education and another led training sessions about special educational needs for teachers in mainstream schools.

LEA adviser/consultant working with the teaching team

LEA advisers had close links with most primary schools and they or consultants were used to:

- initiate a focused CPD activity linked to the school development plan (SDP)

- discuss colleagues' work as part of the annual review process

- provide literacy training in various forms, such as resources and discussion opportunities.

Some primary schools used private consultants alongside LEA advisers. This was usually when there was no adviser available in the subject area or when the support was considered to be inadequate. Alternatively, some consultants had a national credibility or reputation or were personally recommended.

In secondary schools, advisers were brought in to:

- support numeracy across the curriculum

- work with teachers on closure days.

In special schools, advisers and consultants provided:

- specialist training, such as in the use of Makaton or British Sign Language (BSL), or on the needs of pupils with autism

- subject-focused training adapted for special educational needs

- training to use specialised machines to support children's learning.

Overall, secondary school staff were less likely to involve advisers or consultants in school than special or primary schools

4.2.2 CPD activities when children are in school

When teachers had non-contact time and when CPD providers were able to offer CPD activities during school time, demonstration lessons and observation in the school were possible and considered to be a valuable part of professional development. Sometimes there were opportunities for teachers to observe in different schools.

Non-contact time

Activities undertaken during the school day, when teachers were not teaching, varied from informal discussion and support during break times, to more focused and purposeful discussion, for example in mentoring NQTs and students (see Table 4.6).

Primary teachers had less time away from the classroom than secondary teachers. In some primary schools, the headteacher provided cover, or a deputy with a lighter teaching load could release teachers to undertake their coordinator duties. Timetabled non-contact time in secondary schools provided opportunities for teachers' professional development to take place. Special schools had little time to enable staff groups to meet together, although staff said informal discussions about children's needs took place on a continuing basis. Table 4.6 shows the kind of CPD activities undertaken in non-contact time.

Table 4.6   CPD activities undertaken in non-contact time

Time provided	Types of activity		
	Primary	**Secondary**	**Special**
Non-contact time	• staff working in partnership/ teamwork, e.g. mentoring, year group partnerships • organising and arranging training for others • working with HEI with teacher training students • mentoring NQTs	• talking together in year groups in planning or moderating meetings • inducting new staff into schemes of work • introducing exam syllabus • mentoring NQTs	not mentioned

Based on seven primary schools and two secondary schools

Demonstration lessons

Demonstration lessons were given by LEA advisers or consultants and subject coordinators in some primary schools. In primary schools, they often constituted part of the National Literacy Strategy training, in which case they were provided by the LEA adviser and supported by the language coordinator. In other primary schools, subject coordinators gave demonstration lessons for less confident staff. Occasionally, teachers gave demonstration lessons in other schools, or other school staff observed a demonstration lesson in the school of the interviewee, for example a lesson taught by a mathematics lead teacher. Consultants gave demonstration lessons in primary schools to support monitoring, to raise standards or to initiate a focused activity.

Where advisers and consultants gave a demonstration lesson, it added to their credibility as a training provider.

Secondary schools used demonstration lessons less often as professional development activity. However, in one secondary school, where there was a strong training focus, demonstration lessons were provided as part of the initial teacher training programme in school and as part of NQT mentoring. In another secondary school, they were used to share good practice.

In the special schools in the case studies, none of the interviewees suggested that demonstration lessons were part of their professional development activities, although one subject coordinator had used a video to share practice with others. She explained that:

when staff were not always convinced that a change in practice was appropriate, in her coordinator role she decided to use a video of her own lesson to demonstrate how things might be organised. The speech therapist was available to help make the video. The staff then watched the video and were able to see the effects of changes in practice so that they had a clearer picture of what her intentions were.

Observation

In addition to demonstration lessons, observation of fellow teachers was often part of a CPD activity (see Table 4.7).

Different models of observation could be identified:

- a coordinator observing the class teacher with his/her own class

- a class teacher observing the coordinator with his/her own class

- a class teacher observing the coordinator teaching the class teacher's class.

Table 4.7   CPD activities in which observation played a part

Activity	Primary	Secondary	Special
Observation	• the review process • the audit to monitor provision in the school • the NQT induction year where the mentor observed the NQT teaching and the NQT observed other teachers in their classrooms • part of a project being undertaken, e.g. IQEA and SFA (see Appendix A4.4)	• the sharing of good practice • cluster arrangements and work with feeder schools encouraged observation of colleagues in different schools	• observation by the LSA of teachers working with groups of children so that there was continuity of experiences for the children • a video enhanced observation of teaching so that the coordinator was able to introduce new ideas

Based on eight primary schools, two secondary schools and one special school.

Other CPD activities when children were in school

Other activities identified by primary teachers as taking place when children were in school included: working with different year groups, exchanging classes and scrutinising children's work across year groups. These activities allowed teachers to extend the range of their teaching experiences.

One teacher also suggested that listening to children contributed to her professional development because it enabled her to understand them better and therefore to adopt suitable teaching strategies.

In both primary and secondary schools, developing and writing policy and other documents were seen to contribute to professional development.

4.3 School-focused but externally based activities

CPD activities were usually related to the SDP, but some required support from outside agencies and/or attendance by staff at a different venue.

4.3.1 Special projects

All school types had special projects with a clear focus on teaching and learning. In addition, primary and secondary schools organised activities to develop subject expertise (see Table 4.8). IQEA was one example that illustrated the partnerships developed by HEIs and LEAs. This type of provision encourages action research/reflection/enquiry on school-based issues. Details of the projects and teachers' comments are included in Appendix A4.4.

Table 4.8   Special CPD projects in which schools were involved

Activity	Primary	Secondary	Special
Special projects with teaching and learning focus	• IQEA • IIP • PSHE • NOF • nurture groups • SFA • Aiming High • First Steps • Healthy School	• IQEA • IIP • NOF • learning/mentor training • Beacon status • links with industry	• TEACH • EDY • BSL • Makaton • communication day • developing the skills needed to physically move children with physical disability. The LSA talked to the staff in school. • training by the suppliers of some of the specialist machines in use by the children • a sensory course led by a consultant • organising a bereavement counselling course
Subject-related activities	• coordinator training • literacy and numeracy	• CASE (Cognitive Acceleration in Science Education)	

4.3.2 Further professional study

About a quarter of the interviewees in the case study schools were undertaking further professional study leading to first degrees, diplomas and higher degrees (see Appendix A4.5).

Even though distance learning programmes for teachers are marketed online, only one interviewee mentioned a course with a distance learning component. This was provided by an HEI at some distance from the school. This teacher was supported by the LEA but, even so, found the commitment challenging because it entailed studying in the evening after a day teaching. Those on the Learning Support Assistant (LSA) course commented that it was very time-consuming: even if some of the work was undertaken in the classroom, it was still in addition to their normal duties. Most participants appreciated courses that had a practical approach and the opportunity to relate ideas to their school environment. Discussion and sharing ideas with other practitioners was also an influential part of their diploma or degree.

In one primary school and one special school, an HEI delivered lectures in school once a week. All but one of the staff interviewed were involved at different stages of a Master's programme which:

*   supported teachers in changing direction (for one teacher it provided her with the opportunity to pursue a route toward becoming an educational psychologist)

*   broadened teachers' view of education

*   helped teachers to take on additional responsibility that required additional skills.

4.3.3 Management and leadership

Almost half of the interviewees were part of the senior management team (SMT) or had a post of responsibility such as head of department, subject coordinator or key stage manager. Nevertheless, there was a tendency for them to identify CPD activities that focused on teaching and learning rather than on management training. Eight headteachers, five deputies and two teachers in the 18 case study schools mentioned CPD activities relating to management or leadership (see Table 4.9).

Table 4.9   Management and leadership identified by school staff

Primary	Secondary	Special
Headteachers		
• Preparing for OFSTED • OFSTED training • OFSTED • Leadership Programme for Serving Headteachers (LPSH) • LEA courses • Heads you Win project • Local businesses – for interview techniques and management structures	• HEI • Contributing to courses and conferences for headteachers within the LEA • Support network within the authority	• LEA courses • LPSH

(Table 4.9 continued overleaf)

Table 4.9 (continued)

Primary	Secondary	Special
Deputies		
• LEA courses • Headteacher support • NPQH	• NVQ programmes • MBA • NPQH	• LEA courses
Other staff		
• MA	• Post of responsibility	–

Primary schools

Preparation for OFSTED was considered by one primary headteacher to offer good training for headship. The need to write policies when s/he was new to the post had enabled the school to develop a strong staff team. OFSTED training was valuable to help the headteacher know what was expected of, and required by, an inspection team.

Other primary headteachers worked with the LEA to deliver management training. One had attended a leadership course and was now part of a trial for training senior management teams within the LEA, and another led training for other headteachers on formulating the SDP, calculating costs and prioritising CPD.

Two headteachers were involved in an action research project, 'Heads You Win'. It aimed to develop leadership skills, extend understanding and use of action research methods, and provide opportunities to develop and disseminate effective practice in a local context and on a broader scale. One headteacher undertook an in-depth study of the role of the headteacher, and in particular her role in her own school.

Another headteacher had used business contacts to develop the management systems in her school. She had contacted and visited a local supermarket to observe the systems they had in place and used a representative from a chain store to provide training in interview techniques.

Primary deputies identified LEA activities such as deputy support groups, deputy conferences and involvement with NPQH. One of the most frequently mentioned opportunities was the support headteachers provided by working closely with them in school.

Only one teacher in a primary school commented that management training was part of her professional development. It was a selected element of her MA which she felt would give her the opportunity to develop her middle management skills.

Secondary schools

Two secondary schools used NVQs to support management training. One school developed the management teams at different levels, with the SMT working at level 4 and the middle management working at level 3. In another, the deputy headteacher and CPD coordinator felt that she would benefit from understanding what was involved in the qualification being undertaken by non-teaching staff.

Special schools

Special school headteachers identified the LEA and LPSH as contributors to their management development. One special school deputy gained insight into headship by deputising for the headteacher, as well as from the deputy headteacher support network within the LEA. He had also attended a one-day course and an after-school session on performance management and the role of the deputy head.

4.4 School involvement in LEA-wide CPD activities

Primary, secondary and special schools identified LEA-wide activities and initiatives in which they were involved.

4.4.1 LEA networks

Headteachers in all sectors were appreciative of:

- local networks and informal contacts

- pyramid and cluster group activities

- strategic management groups.

Primary subject coordinators and secondary heads of department identified useful networks and support groups including:

- LEA courses for subject coordinators across the LEA; in primary schools, the focus was often on literacy and numeracy

- LEA-organised key stage support groups and courses.

In four of the LEAs in the case study areas, cluster group activities linked schools in a close geographical location or linked primary schools to a secondary school. This enabled teachers to develop skills as part of their professional development. In one school, the CPD coordinator talked about a project which developed direct links for children in liaison between primary and secondary schools. The primary children were required to work on a science activity in a book, which they took with them to continue work in their secondary school. Originally teachers had met together three times a year, but now they met more often and shared subject knowledge. This had led to extending the idea to different subject areas.

Other support groups emerged when teachers engaged in an activity focusing on a shared interest. For example, NQT induction activities encouraged professional dialogue between mentors and NQTs. A steering group for a research project encouraged teachers to share experiences, and self-help groups had developed and been maintained over a period of time.

4.4.2 Other CPD activities

Survey respondents and interviewees mentioned a range of other CPD activities.

Conferences

One-off conferences featured highly as CPD activities in the responses to the LEA and school surveys. In the case study schools, however, only four headteachers, two deputies and five other teachers mentioned conferences as contributing to their professional development. This amounted to 11 out of 81 interviewees. Sometimes conferences were part of a wider programme of study and sometimes they were a stimulus for participation in a special project. Two secondary headteachers and one primary school deputy mentioned residential conferences. Other interviewees referred to courses but did not use the term 'conference'.

Individual teachers mentioned a range of other activities that contributed to their professional development. Details are given below.

Study abroad

Some primary headteachers and teachers, and one secondary teacher, had travelled abroad as part of a special project.

One headteacher mentioned that her deputy had undertaken study abroad as part of the Teachers' International Professional Development (TIPD) programme. The deputy, when interviewed, talked mainly about CPD activities in school and then went on to explain about a study week in Canada. The suggestion for participation in this initiative had come from the headteacher. The deputy headteacher commented that overseas study had been possible for her because she did not have family commitments.

The study involved identifying a clear focus and objectives; she selected boys' achievement in literacy at KS1. She was required to plan and evaluate her study/project and to produce a report for the LEA director. The experience had enabled her to:

* work with teachers from another country

* develop links within the LEA and across LEAs

* implement ideas in school – she is now working on family literacy issues in the local area

* develop e-mail pals and pen pals.

Going abroad had had an impact on her teaching, by giving her:

- a more positive approach to teaching

- increased respect for adults and children

- recognition that celebration and using praise were important

- a wider perspective about teaching and education.

Using video

One primary school planned to make a CPD video linked to a training package to focus on teaching and learning. The intention was that teachers would watch and evaluate lessons on the video, share their views with other teachers, and come up with their own 'inspection report'.

Another primary school had found the National Numeracy Strategy training video a valuable resource.

A third example was:

a language coordinator who had been in post for about a year. She had to demonstrate practice to advisers, to convince the teachers that the Literacy Hour could be incorporated into their existing framework. The video was shown to teachers, and the language coordinator was there to answer questions about her practice. This had given her confidence and made her more secure in her own knowledge base. She felt that it was successful because she had put it into practice. She had used the video with different groups and each time had given her greater confidence.

Individual school CPD activities

In some cases, individual school personnel identified specific CPD activities but they did not describe them in detail. One primary headteacher had used a private IT company to provide EXCEL training. The school now used EXCEL to produce data- tracking sheets for English and maths.

Other primary schools had developed e-mail links with other schools and used the internet to access information and to keep up to date.

One teacher attended a practical activity funded by the Arts Council and provided by the National Orchestra, which had enabled her to develop a music scheme in school. She hoped, as a follow-up, to work with the National Orchestra in school.

Depending upon their role and responsibility in school, other teachers attended activities on first aid and child protection. Governor training was available for teacher governors. One secondary teacher felt that her involvement with the teacher union contributed to her professional development.

4.5 Summary

◆ Interviewees represented a range of length of service and number of years in post, but no clear picture emerged to suggest that teachers at different stages of their career are more or less likely to become involved in professional development.

◆ Similar CPD activities were identified by secondary, primary and special schools, although staff in secondary schools felt that closure days were particularly useful. Primary schools were more likely to use demonstration lessons and observation of colleagues.

◆ Cluster groups and networks were appreciated by teachers in all types of schools but particularly by secondary headteachers, heads of department and primary subject coordinators.

◆ Primary schools focused on literacy and numeracy CPD activities, and ICT training was in evidence in both primary and secondary schools. Special schools focused on developing their special educational needs expertise.

◆ Most of the activities described by interviewees had a teaching and learning focus. Even the management teams who undertook some management training identified activities that were related to teaching and learning.

◆ Study abroad, use of videos and governor training were mentioned by a few interviewees.

◆ There was a wide range of activities available for teachers and they had a varied focus. The school, usually, had a leading role in determining the focus and the nature of the activity. The LEA played a significant part in supporting school strategies, and in providing and facilitating CPD activities.

5. PROCESSES

This chapter identifies and discusses the processes that govern teachers' participation in continuing professional development (CPD) activities. Three core processes will be addressed in turn: how CPD needs are identified, school procedures for teachers participating in CPD activities, and how CPD is evaluated.

5.1 Need identification

This section will discuss the process of need identification as revealed by the LEA questionnaires and interviews, the school questionnaires, and the case study interviews with staff.

5.1.1 LEA findings

LEA questionnaire respondents were asked to indicate the methods used in their authority to identify the CPD needs of teachers. LEAs made a response to this question by choosing from a list of predetermined methods provided in the questionnaire (see Table 5.1). Only one LEA in the sample did not respond to this question.

Table 5.1   Range of methods used by LEAs to support CPD needs of teachers

Methods used	Frequency of response
Application of national policies	102
Response to Education Development Plan targets and actions	102
Consultation with link advisers	97
Response to special requests made directly to LEA	94
Liaison with school staff development coordinators	89
Review of School Development Plan targets and actions	85
Questionnaires to teachers	43
Other methods (meetings, discussions)	16
No response from LEA	1
Total	629

Based on 105 LEAs. Respondents could give more than one response

When these national frequencies were analysed by the type of LEA, the numbers involved and the results obtained were neither surprising nor illuminating. For example, new authorities were least likely to use liaison with school staff development coordinators as a form of identifying CPD needs. This may be because the relationships required to make it an effective method of identifying need were not in place at that time.

The most popular methods were the application of national policies and response to Education Development Plan (EDP) targets and actions (102 responses each). For example, at the time of the NFER study, LEAs nationwide were commonly providing literacy and numeracy training to address the National Literacy and Numeracy Strategies (see Chapter 4).

Interviews with LEA advisers provided insight into the role of the LEA in responding to the EDP targets and action, as part of the need identification process. The EDP was seen as a tool to identify the package of courses that should be provided by the LEA. Two LEA advisers reported that the EDP should ideally be drawn up in consultation with schools and informed by their School Development Plans (SDP), as this allowed a local flavour to be incorporated into the overall principles and requirements. Reviewing the SDP targets and action was also a frequent response in the LEA questionnaire (85 responses). Thus, the EDP and the SDP were key tools to identify the national and local school requirements. These Plans were then used to inform the CPD activities provided by the LEA to schools, via their programme of courses.

Consultation with link advisers, liaison with staff development coordinators and LEA responses to special requests were also common responses in the LEA questionnaire. These methods provide a more direct and immediate way of identifying CPD needs, operating via interactions between the LEA (advisers) and schools (CPD coordinator), rather than via documentation.

In the LEA interviews, advisers spoke about the relationship between their teams and schools. One adviser saw his role as using data from classroom observations, working with schools on their planning and delivery, and through joint evaluation to identify needs. Another adviser described a review process whereby the LEA audited a school to identify and celebrate good practice.

There is also a central role played by the school in the need identification process. One adviser explained:

> *Schools are better able to undertake this task, as they have a clearer understanding of the relationship between school and individual needs. They can identify need, match need and see how it affects their practice. It is the responsibility of the CPD coordinator and the leadership group within the school to undertake this task. They need to be approachable.*

The CPD coordinator was viewed to be in the best position to identify the particular needs of the school and individual staff members, and to request CPD accordingly. It was the school's responsibility to identify and match CPD needs appropriately. These comments essentially highlight the need for effective communication and coordination between the school and the LEA, so that CPD needs can be identified and addressed appropriately. This issue appears central to facilitating all the methods reported above.

5.1.2 School questionnaire findings

Respondents were asked to indicate how their school identified teachers' CPD needs. Schools in all LEAs made a response to this question by choosing from a list of predetermined methods provided in the questionnaire (see Table 5.2a).

Table 5.2(a)   Range of methods used by schools to identify teachers' CPD needs

Methods used	Frequency of response
Application of national policies	42
Review of School Development Plan	42
Response to OFSTED Inspection/Action Plan	37
Performance Management Process	31
Suggestions from LEA Link Adviser	24
Response to LEA EDP	23
Involvement with Investors in People	16
Other	22
Total	237

Based on 42 schools. Respondents could give more than one response.

Where 'other' methods were indicated, 22 schools mentioned a total of 30 strategies (see Table 5.2b). The most common methods indicated by schools were the application of national policies and review of the SDP (42 responses each). These findings are similar to the most frequent LEA responses, discussed in the previous section. Schools also indicated that they used the outcomes of their OFSTED inspection and the Performance Management process to identify CPD needs.

Table 5.2(b) Other methods of identifying CPD needs

Other methods	Frequency of response
Individual staff needs/interest	7
Regular career interview/discussion	6
New staff induction	4
Department improvement plans	2
Active link to a network of schools	2
In-house training to ensure course continuity	1
Everyday need, e.g. first aid, child protection	1
Line management suggestions	1
Training for IT	1
Involvement in initiatives	1
Local/town initiatives	1
Audits carried out by consultants	1
Other – unspecified	2
Total	30

Based on 22 schools. Respondents could give more than one response.

5.1.3 Case study interviews

In the case study interviews, staff were asked a series of questions to ascertain their experiences of CPD activities. These included: need identification processes, procedures for staff's participation in CPD; how staff found out about activities; how easy it was to organise, and what happened upon completion.

Table 5.3 shows the range of need identification processes reported in the case study interviews and the frequency of mention by school type (primary, secondary, special school).

As can be seen, there are a wide range of need identification processes that reveal the CPD needs of the school as a whole, and those of individual staff members.

School Development Plan

The headteacher, deputy headteacher and/or CPD coordinator in all the schools mentioned the importance of the SDP to prioritising and directing their training needs. However, in some schools all staff interviewed reported this, indicating a wider awareness and focus upon the school's development needs and priorities.

Two schools (one primary and one secondary from different local authorities) indicated that they had become involved in IQEA (Improving the Quality of Education for All), an initiative based upon teaching and learning styles, as it matched the aims of their School Development Plan and the school's philosophy. Their responses illustrate how the SDP had directed the school's involvement in a specific initiative:

> *Became involved with IQEA initiative as it matched two out of three aims of the SDP. It suited the school philosophy, as they* [the school] *wanted to develop teaching and learning.*
>
> (Secondary headteacher)

The SDP is used to prioritise areas for CPD and it is also one of the major factors that determines staff involvement in CPD activities (see section 5.2). An emerging theme, which seems to underpin the school's ethos and emphasis placed upon the importance of professional development, is the fundamental role of the headteacher: his or her views of the importance of professional development are embedded within the school culture, and this emphasis is incorporated within the SDP:

> *The SDP highlights training issues and priority areas that will be costed out and drive the budget. PD is a priority area and an integral part of school development.* (Primary headteacher)

Table 5.3   Need identification processes reported in the case study interviews

Need identification processes	Details	Frequency of response by school type		
		Primary N = 12	Secondary N = 3	Special N = 3
School Development Plan	• prioritisation/ identification of CPD needs of schools • directs CPD	12	3	3
Appraisal	• 1:1 appraisal • staff reviews • professional development interview	8	2	2
Performance Management interviews	• formalised appraisal	7	3	3
Lesson/subject monitoring	• classroom observations • analysis of results	6	1	1
OFSTED Report	• inspection report identifies need	5	–	1
Links with other schools	• visits to identify effective CPD in other schools • meetings to identify INSET needs	4	–	2
Staff meetings/ discussions	• brainstorming of CPD priorities	3	2	1
Government	• identification of national priorities/ CPD needs	3	1	1
Questionnaires	• distribution to identify need	3	–	1
NQT Appraisal	• identification of training needs	1	–	–
Team residential/ away day	• staff identify what needs to be done	–	1	–
Investors in People	• indicate CPD need	–	1	–
LEA	• the LEA directs CPD priorities and needs	–	–	1

Appraisal and Performance Management

Appraisal and Performance Management were the next most frequently cited ways of identifying CPD needs within schools. The appraisal process tended to comprise one-to-one staff reviews, discussions or interviews. These tended to be fairly informal, where staff discussed their strengths and weaknesses usually with the headteacher or someone from the senior management team.

One primary school provided an example:

Staff undertake a yearly professional development discussion with the headteacher. Before the discussion, they complete a questionnaire which asks a range of questions regarding their working experiences. In particular, it asks staff how they would like to develop professionally, change their responsibilities, objectives they would like to set themselves, their career aspirations and so on. Questions concerning the school's objectives (e.g. targets for SDP, vision for development of the school building) are asked, and an evaluation of school issues and targets is also requested. This questionnaire then forms the basis of discussion in the one-to-one appraisal with the headteacher, and it also informs the School Development Plan

This process appears useful as it enables individual staff to focus upon their own CPD needs as well as the overall priorities of the school. Alongside the appraisal process, staff mentioned Performance Management as a more formalised process of need identification. A few concerns were expressed that this process would be tied to performance-related pay.

Monitoring

Staff in the three school types also mentioned lesson/subject monitoring as a fairly common way of identifying CPD needs. Staff reported being observed whilst teaching, and having their pupils' performance results examined, in order to identify CPD areas that required further development. Typically, this process would be conducted or overseen by the subject coordinator.

Need for CPD is identified by in-school monitoring; teachers are observed and given feedback from their lessons. This can be stressful, but now the school is moving toward specialist teaching where subject coordinators will lead on lessons. (Primary teacher)

Other methods

Other approaches to need identification mentioned less frequently were:

- issues identified from OFSTED reports

- links with other schools, where collaborative meetings helped to identify common needs

- staff meetings, where discussions yielded CPD needs

- questionnaires.

It was also interesting to note the frustrations expressed by a few of the interviewees that the school did not play as big a role as they would have liked in identifying and prioritising their CPD as, in their view, the Government dictated this. Similarly, staff in one special school mentioned that the LEA directed the CPD priorities.

Key players

Throughout the interviews, key people within and connected to the school were identified as playing a major role in identifying CPD needs (see Table 5.4).

Table 5.4   Key players in the need identification process reported in the case study interviews

Key players in identifying need	Details	Frequency of response by school type		
		Primary N = 12	Secondary N = 3	Special N = 3
Individual identification	• individuals identify their own needs • self-evaluation	9	2	1
Subject coordinators/ heads of faculty	• identify training needs • observations	6	1	1
LEA adviser	• reviews/ visits to help school identify CPD direction • identify objectives in preparation for training • observations • aware of school needs/local context	6	–	2
Headteacher	• identifies CPD priorities	3	2	1
CPD coordinator	• pulls all the information together to identify key priorities	2	1	1
Senior management team	• identify training needs of all staff	1	2	1
Line manager	• discuss career development	–	2	–
Governors	• identify priority areas	–	1	1
Staff Development Committee	• draw up policy, allocate funds	–	1	–
Consultant advice	• bring in external consultant	–	1	–

As can be seen, staff frequently mentioned that they identified their own CPD needs and sought training accordingly. The subject coordinator/head of faculty was also identified as influential to this process by carrying out classroom observations, having discussions with staff about their training needs, and viewing lesson plans, which highlighted areas that needed to be developed.

LEA advisers were also seen to aid the need identification and prioritisation process. Primary and special schools mentioned their involvement through visits to the school to undertake reviews or classroom observations. Additionally, LEA advisers often visited the school to identify objectives that needed to be specifically addressed and covered in their delivery of a specific CPD activity. Or the LEA adviser would use this background to inform the LEA programme of courses to be offered. Either way, this process was viewed as most useful when the LEA adviser was seen to have an awareness of the school's need and the local context.

> *The subject coordinator* [communications] *has discussions with staff about their professional development. They identify needs; look at SDP and subject development plans.*
> (Special school teacher)

> *LEA provides termly reviews to help schools identify their CPD direction. They offer staff evaluation and advisory support. There is a good relationship with adviser.* (Primary headteacher)

> *LEA adviser discusses needs in advance of training; they* [LEA advisers] *identify objectives and come up with ideas to fit what is happening.* (Primary teacher)

> *LEA advisers are aware of national and local context – this leads to targeted training.* (Primary deputy headteacher)

The headteacher, CPD coordinator and the senior management team were also seen, to a lesser extent, to be involved in the identification of school CPD priorities. However, there was a stronger involvement by the headteacher and the CPD coordinator than specifically mentioned in this context: these were the key people who reported consulting the School Development Plan to identify the CPD needs of the school.

As suggested earlier, it seems clear that a lively school culture and a positive attitude towards professional development stem from the enthusiasm of the headteacher. Both heads and other staff cited the influence of the headteacher upon the school's attitude to professional development.

> *Learning is a high priority in the school and, personally, for myself, I relish change and being at the forefront of education, as this is a powerful tool for development. Involvement has snowballed…CPD is a priority and non-contact time is offered. Professional development is a priority area – it is an integral part of school development.* (Primary headteacher)

In several schools, this enthusiasm for CPD permeated throughout the school and was at the heart of the school's professional development culture. The attitude of the headteacher appeared fundamental in determining the priority that the school placed upon CPD and the type of activities that they become involved in.

5.2 School procedure

This section discusses the school procedure for staff participation in CPD activities. The questionnaires (LEA and school) did not ask respondents to provide information about the school procedure. However, the case study interviews reveal an in-depth insight into the process of staff awareness and factors that determined their participation in CPD (see Table 5.5).

Table 5.5 **School procedure to become involved in CPD activities reported in the case study interviews**

Procedures	Details	Frequency of response by school type		
		Primary N = 12	Secondary N = 3	Special N = 3
1. Finding out about CPD activities				
LEA book circulated	• staff view CPD courses on offer • express an interest in particular CPD	9	1	3
LEA advisers	• suggest and recommend CPD activities	5	–	1
Subject coordinator	• highlights/suggests CPD for staff	3	–	–
Courses advertised	• box containing course information accessible to all in staff room • school notice board	1	1	2
Individuals	• instigate own CPD exploration – find out about courses, e.g. in magazines, word of mouth	1	1	1

(Table 5.5 continued overleaf)

Table 5.5(continued)

		Frequency of response by school type		
Procedures	**Details**	**Primary** N = 12	**Secondary** N = 3	**Special** N = 3
2. Processes				
Role of headteacher	• distributes information to staff • finds out about/ instigates CPD • suggests CPD to staff/makes recommendations • organises CPD	12	2	2
Role of CPD coordinator	• receives CPD information • circulates information to staff • suggests CPD activities to staff/ makes recommendations • books staff on CPD/ signs course application form • makes final decision	10	3	3
Application form	• reasons for taking part • impact upon teaching and learning	3	3	2
Role of head of faculty/ department	• signs course application form • passes on CPD information	–	2	-
3. Factors that determine staff participation in CPD				
SDP criteria	• CPD that meets school's need is prioritised • balance agreed between SDP and individual need	7	3	2
Funding availability	• linkages to SDP required • funding criteria set	4	3	2
Supply cover	• availability • suitability	3	3	2
Relevance of course	• applicability • justification of CPD	2	–	1
Order of application	• first come, first served basis	–	–	1

Table 5.5(continued)

It should be noted that the procedures for staff to apply to participate in CPD activities were in fact clearer for external activities, offered by the LEA, than for in-school CPD.

The roles of headteacher and the CPD coordinator were central to staff's participation in CPD activities. Ultimately they were the 'gatekeepers' to the school's involvement in CPD activities; they were most likely to receive the LEA book of activities and other course information from universities or organisations. They then either distributed this information amongst staff, so that the full range of CPD activities could be viewed and preferences expressed, and/or they selected and recommended CPD activities to staff. The research indicates that both of these procedures were taking place within the schools.

The CPD coordinator and headteacher talk together and agree which courses/activity staff should do. (Primary CPD coordinator).

I look through the red book, identify courses and see if they would have any merit for that person that wants to be involved or point them in the right direction if they have not already seen it. They usually take up the course. In the past, it has been a democratic decision; the book had gone around the school and teachers could choose. Now, they need to fit in the scheme of things and funding.
(Primary CPD coordinator)

The headteacher and the staff development officer look at courses that are relevant for the school, having looked at the staff audit, and suggest that teachers need to do particular courses – focused and targeted. (Primary CPD coordinator)

When the LEA course information was distributed, staff had an opportunity to view all the external CPD activities that were on offer and to indicate a preference for particular activities. This was a fairly popular approach within the three school types. Other, less frequently mentioned methods were via the LEA adviser or subject coordinators, who suggested and highlighted to staff the specific activities which they felt would most meet their needs.

Information from LEA is circulated to staff. Individuals identify their particular interest in a course or training and apply on the pink course application form. The CPD coordinators then identify and prioritise the applications.
(Special school deputy headteacher)

Staff are given a list of LEA activities every half year; they make four choices and prioritise those which they think will be most helpful and valuable. (Special school nursery nurse)

It was interesting to note comments regarding the appropriateness of the LEA courses. Primary and secondary school staff only occasionally indicated that LEA courses were not always suitable to the current CPD needs of the school. However, staff in the special schools commented that this was often the case for them and that, on the whole, the LEA courses were not specialised enough to meet their needs. As an alternative, they sought more appropriate courses from specialist organisations:

Often LEA courses are ineffective, as they do not address the specialist training that the school requires.
(Special school headteacher)

The LEA often cannot provide specialist courses. Thus, specialist training links are needed with organisations such as Mencap and the Autistic Society. (Special school headteacher)

LEA courses often are not orientated toward special needs.
(Special school teacher)

LEA courses tended to be most effective for special schools when the LEA advisory team were aware of, and receptive to, the school's needs.

LEA courses are often good, as the advisers know the staff and the population of the children. (Special school teacher)

There are problems with LEA courses as they are not specialist enough. However, they [the advisers] *are approachable and aid with information finding.* (Special school teacher)

LEA put on a wide and varied programme – of high quality. The advisory team really listens to the feedback to analyse the courses and conferences that are needed in the future. They also keep in tune with school needs and demands. They are quick in developing Government initiatives. (Special school CPD coordinator)

The CPD coordinator and the headteacher also played a key role in organising the CPD activities for staff and made the ultimate decision as to whether activities were appropriate. The MORI survey of CPD findings (1995) was summarised as: 'Continuing professional development (CPD) currently in place in most schools appears to operate on an *ad hoc* basis with no real linkages across school development planning, personal development planning and teachers' appraisals.' This highlights the difficulties in implementing a balance between school and individual teachers' CPD needs. However, the NFER project reveals that the CPD coordinator decided whether the CPD activity would meet the needs of the school, the aims and priorities identified in the SDP, and the needs of individual staff. Staff in all school types frequently cited the importance of the headteacher and the CPD coordinator in the procedures for CPD participation. Two of the three secondary schools mentioned that the head of faculty might also perform this role alongside the head and CPD coordinator.

The CPD coordinator highlights courses available and helps teachers to bridge initiatives between their own demands and the school. [He/she] *makes sure that staff have opportunities for financial support by prioritising needs.*
(Special school CPD coordinator)

Staff can make a preference, approach the CPD coordinator; involvement will depend upon the school priorities in the School Development Plan.   (Primary teacher)

The headteacher is sent the LEA portfolio of courses; the university also sends out a timetable of courses. If these are not appropriate, then the headteacher will seek elsewhere, e.g. IiP [Investors in People], NAHT [National Association of Headteachers]. CPD needs to fit with the school's priorities.
                                                          (Primary headteacher)

Once needs have been identified, she will approach the CPD coordinator; there is then a balance between school and personal needs – if you can justify doing a course, you usually get to do it. The CPD coordinator fills in the application. She will also make suggestions about the course.   (Primary SENCO)

Once CPD activities were identified, some schools reported using an application form (for external and internal courses) which required staff to indicate why they were applying for the course and how it would impact upon teaching and learning. Such forms appear valuable to focus the perceived usefulness and benefits of the CPD: how it will meet the needs of the school and teachers' individual needs. For example, one special school asked staff to identify two or three targets that they hoped to be able to put into practice after the course, and whether they would be willing/able to provide a post-training session. Typically, the headteacher and/or the CPD coordinator would sign off this form. This decision tended to be mediated by several factors. The main mediating factor was whether the CPD met the school's priorities, as identified in the SDP (see Table 5.5).

In choosing CPD activities, staff were often mindful of the school's priorities and needs, as these would ultimately decide whether they would be allowed to participate. Occasionally they needed to justify the relevance of the course.

It is the culture of the school to think in terms of the SDP. If it fits into SDP, then it is readily organised.
                                            (Primary deputy headteacher)

Teachers decide what they want and it needs to reflect what the school needs. They can meet personal needs as long as they can show that it is going to move the school on. They approach the CPD coordinator, who decides if their needs can be met within the school or by a course.   (Primary CPD coordinator)

Funding and staffing issues were linked to the focus upon the SDP. There were often difficulties with the suitability and availability of supply cover. Furthermore, staff commented that they still needed to prepare lesson plans for supply staff. This appeared less of an issue in schools where the headteacher covered lessons, or where staff in small, team-orientated schools arranged for one another.

Supply cover is an increasing problem because teachers are not available – recruitment and retention issues.

(Primary headteacher)

Supply is not an issue as the headteacher acts as supply cover to keep costs down.

(Primary headteacher)

If CPD fits in with SDP, then it's OK. CPD coordinator controls the funding, has an overview and distributes funding – linked to SDP.

(Secondary teacher)

Courses are always linked to SDP, which is the highest priority. Course refusal may happen if supply cover cannot be arranged.

(Primary CPD coordinator)

5.3 Evaluation/feedback

This section discusses what happens following CPD, as revealed by the LEA questionnaires, the school questionnaires and the case study interviews with staff.

5.3.1 LEA findings

LEA respondents were asked to select from a list the methods used for the evaluation of CPD activities. The four categories of evaluation listed were:

- self-report questionnaires

- structured verbal feedback

- informal discussions

- progress reports.

Overall, the most frequent method of evaluation was self-report questionnaires (667 responses), followed by informal discussions (548 responses), then structured verbal feedback (437), with the least favoured method being the progress report (304).

However, certain methods of evaluation were deemed more appropriate for certain activities. For example, the most popular method of evaluation for action research was progress reports (47 responses), whereas the most popular method for evaluating observation of colleagues was structured verbal feedback (62 responses). Further details of the responses elicited from this question are given below in Table 5.6. Where frequencies were analysed by type of LEA, Welsh respondents preferred structured verbal feedback and progress reports for all types of CPD activity, while counties tended to prefer self-report questionnaires, especially for one-off conferences, action research and higher academic and professional courses.

LEAs were invited to give details about other CPD activities and evaluation methods. Other methods of evaluation referred to: follow-up course evaluation, publications/website, and reviews of in-school development.

Table 5.6   Methods used for evaluating CPD activities

ACTIVITY	Frequency of response to multiple-choice items:			
	Self-report questionnaire	Structured verbal feedback	Informal discussions	Progress report
One-off conferences	101	31	48	11
One-off seminars	96	22	44	5
One-off workshops	98	23	42	6
Ongoing non-accredited	77	27	35	24
In-school training	66	34	57	21
Networking forums	37	28	52	14
Action research	28	25	26	47
Accredited higher academic	39	28	24	27
Accredited higher/professional	44	28	28	31
In-class support	23	53	52	34
Observing colleagues	17	62	41	40
Mentoring colleagues	17	43	46	26
Visiting other schools	21	31	50	17

Based on 105 LEAs. Respondents could give more than one response.

LEAs were also asked to provide information about ways in which they collected and used the evaluation data to monitor and evaluate the effectiveness of CPD activities. The question was open-ended and therefore generated numerous responses, which were coded and analysed. Many LEAs simply gave further information about the methods used for evaluating CPD activities, whilst others described the way the evaluation data were used to improve CPD provision. Their comments are reported according to those two broad categories.

Further methods for evaluating CPD

Many LEAs used evaluation data to inform bigger, authority-wide evaluations. In response to the open-ended question, 45 respondents indicated that the evaluation data were used for purposes of feedback. In these cases, the LEA synthesised the evaluation data and then reported the results to the CPD provider, the INSET coordinator or professional development groups, thereby allowing each group to interpret them for their own purposes. Twenty-three respondents indicated that the evaluation data were used to inform discussions in meetings or consultative groups, such as networking forums. A further 20 LEAs indicated the data were used in annual reviews, for example in LEAs' annual reports on the achievements of each school; progress was measured against performance indicators identified during the evaluations of CPD activities year-on-year. A further 15 responses described how evaluation data had been used for other reporting purposes, such as case study evaluations describing effective CPD practice.

Use of evaluation data

Respondents outlined a number of strategies to use evaluation data to improve the effectiveness of future CPD. Sixty six LEAs indicated that course providers used data to revise the focus and content of future activities on offer to teachers. The data served a range of other purposes: for example, to revise certain EDP/SDP targets, to follow up particular issues highlighted by evaluations and to monitor subsequent alterations.

5.3.2 School questionnaire findings

The school questionnaire asked respondents to give details about how teachers gave feedback on the quality of the CPD activity. This was an open-ended question and generated a variety of responses that were coded into the categories outlined in Table 5.7.

Table 5.7   Methods of evaluating CPD activities

Evaluation activity	Frequency
Evaluation forms	23
Formal discussions/meetings or presentations	17
Report to CPD coordinator	9
Informal discussions	4
Other	12
Total	65

Based on 42 schools. Respondents could give more than one response.

The most frequent method of evaluation was evaluation forms (23 responses), followed by formal discussions/meetings or presentations (17 responses).

Respondents were further asked to provide information about ways in which they used to monitor and evaluate the effectiveness of CPD activities. This question was open-ended and generated a variety of responses that were coded into the categories shown in Table 5.8.

In some schools, the evaluation feedback was not used at all, whereas in other schools, it was reported that teachers cascaded their experiences to the rest of the school staff. Furthermore, where individual teachers had attended an activity with inspiring speakers, the speakers were then invited to contribute to whole-school activities. In one unusual example, the feedback was used at the governors' team-building weekend. However, no further details were given about this activity.

Table 5.8   Use of feedback about the effectiveness of CPD

How feedback is used	Frequency
For planning future CPD	15
To feed into SDP	10
For dissemination and feedback to staff	10
To have an effect on school policies	9
For management reviews	7
As feedback to providers	4
For annual reviews	3
For reports	1
For miscellaneous purposes	5
Total	66

Based on 42 schools. Respondents could give more than one response.

In many cases, schools commented or implied that the feedback should be available for all staff to view in a central place, and that the feedback was not as systematic or rigorous as the coordinators would have liked. Respondents highlighted that the quality of CPD activities was variable and that the monitoring process should be more structured and organised by systematic recording or by ensuring that the CPD activity was used to identify further action required.

Even though evaluation forms were the most frequently used strategy for monitoring the effectiveness of CPD, they were not always considered to be effective. For example, respondents claimed that evaluation forms were often not completed and, even when they were, the approach was not always successful as it was too bureaucratic. Other respondents gave details about a school response form, which was displayed for all staff to see as an example of an effective feedback strategy. In another case, staff were required to grade activities on a formal, brief paper to ensure quality and value for money, while a small school of three teachers mentioned that they relied on anecdotal staff room chat.

Several respondents described how teachers were asked to fill in school-designed evaluation forms to indicate how worthwhile (or not) courses had been and their intention to implement ideas at class/school level. It is clear that, in these schools, there was an expectation that the CPD activity should/could have an impact on teaching and learning.

5.3.3 Case study interviews

Staff were asked in the case study interviews about any follow-up to CPD activities (see Table 5.9).

Once again, staff mainly focused upon externally provided CPD activities, i.e. what happened on their return to school after attending a course or conference.

Table 5.9   Evaluation/ feedback following CPD reported in the case study interviews

Evaluation	Details	Frequency of response by school type		
		Primary N = 12	Secondary N = 3	Special N = 3
Evaluation form	• complete evaluation form • evaluate CPD to inform future courses • log in staff portfolios	6	1	3
Implement into teaching	• put into practice	6	2	–
Feedback in staff meeting	• staff meeting/ faculty meeting to feedback to staff	5	3	3
Informal feedback amongst staff	• informally share ideas with colleagues	5	–	3
Role of CPD coordinator	• keeps staff portfolios up to date • maintains record of courses/ evaluations • monitors information to inform future CPD	5	3	2
Cascade/distribute materials to staff	• distribute information/ materials	4	1	1
Monitoring of impact	• monitor lessons to evaluate impact	2	1	–
Materials logged	• kept in library • coordinator keeps materials	2	–	1

Table 5.9 reveals that the completion of an evaluation form following CPD was a popular practice within all school types. Several schools provided examples of their evaluation forms. These tended to address: delivery, content, relevance/applicability, whether the course met the stated objectives, whether it was cost-effective/should be attended again. They also requested an evaluation concerning its potential impact on teaching and learning. The

evaluation form appeared a useful tool, as it tended to be kept in staff's professional development portfolios, and it was reported that this could then be referred to in order to assess any impact upon teaching and learning, or to inform future CPD activities. Typically, the CPD coordinator would maintain this information, but one school reported that the LEA adviser used this feedback to keep in touch and up to date with the school's training needs:

> *On return they fill in a sheet and note whether it was worthwhile, if there are any further developments and whether the info needs to be cascaded to other staff. A copy is kept for professional development portfolios.* (Primary teacher)

> *After attending the activity, [staff] tick categories about the quality of the CPD; then after six months they have to say what effect it is having.* (Secondary teacher)

On return from CPD activities, staff also reported that they tended to give feedback within staff meetings, or informally via chats with colleagues. However, once again CPD coordinators played a central role in this school process: they kept staff records, maintained records of attended courses/ evaluations, and monitored all information/feedback to inform future CPD activities:

> *The CPD coordinator manages individual and school balance of CPD; they keep track of who has done what activity, allowing monitoring of who is doing CPD, who doesn't and who needs to do some.* (Special school CPD coordinator)

> *Six months later* [following CPD], *staff are asked for feedback about how they are using it in the classroom. The CPD coordinator uses evidence to reinforce attendance on future courses. There is a form to fill in, to identify additional training required. The CPD coordinator keeps track of good and weak courses. There is a personal file for future records for each individual. Twice a year, there is a summary of courses and areas that have been covered – identifies global issues, impact upon teaching and learning and additional needs. School INSET is monitored through the forms.* (Secondary CPD coordinator)

Clearly, a distinction needs to be made between evaluation of CPD activities and evaluation of their impact upon teaching and learning. Staff tended to report upon what happened, on their return to school, following external CPD. The MORI survey of CPD (1995) reported that few schools had any systematic means of evaluating CPD. They explained that 69 per cent of teachers reported that there were measures in place to evaluate the effectiveness of CPD activities, but, in fact, few specific measures could be specified. The most common response was feedback with either the GEST (Grants for Education Support and Training)/INSET coordinator, mentoring with other staff, debriefing and feedback sessions. MORI argues that these methods are dissemination rather than evaluation.

In the NFER project, it was reported that schools' evaluation forms tended to ask staff how they perceived CPD would impact upon teaching and learning. The CPD coordinator would then refer to this information to assess the impact or to inform future CPD. A few staff reported that they were asked, three to six months later, to evaluate how the CPD activity had impacted upon their teaching and learning. However, it is not clear how this impact would be systematically assessed or evaluated in the long term.

The OFSTED Annual Report (1995/1996) (OFSTED, 1997) stated that long-term evaluation of INSET was generally weak, and that it needed to be more systematic with closer attention to value for money. It suggested that the development of an up-to-date directory on the range and quality of INSET providers would be a useful tool. This would then provide schools with reliable information on which to base their choice of providers in a competitive environment. Although there have been changes in professional development requirements since the mid 1990s, and although short-term evaluations are in place, it would seem that less attention has been given to long-term evaluations.

5.4 Summary of processes and implications

- This chapter has identified and discussed the processes that govern participation in CPD activities by schools and individuals. Throughout the process, key themes have emerged with regard to the cycle of need identification, participation and evaluation of CPD activities. The SDP clearly had a key role in this process: it was used to identify and prioritise CPD (by schools and staff), and determined whether staff participated in chosen CPD activities or not. Thus, a cycle was formed which ultimately hinged upon appropriately identifying and meeting CPD needs, via the SDP.

- The CPD coordinator and/or the headteacher played a central role. They were identified as the 'gatekeepers' to staff's participation in external CPD activities; they received the CPD activities on offer and made suggestions to staff. They ultimately decided staff participation in CPD activities, usually based on whether it would meet the aims of the SDP, and whether funding (dependent upon SDP priorities) and supply cover were available.

- Evaluation forms were a popular method to follow up staff's participation in external CPD activities. Staff tended to evaluate aspects such as the delivery, content and impact that they perceived it would have upon teaching and learning. These forms tended to vary in format and structure: they need to be more systematic, rigorous, and available for all staff to view. Feedback via formal or informal dissemination to colleagues was also a common approach.

♦ Evaluation feedback was utilised by LEAs to inform authority-wide evaluations, and course providers so that the focus and content of future CPD could be revised. Within schools, the CPD coordinator and/or headteacher would maintain, review and monitor this information to inform future CPD participation. Long-term monitoring and evaluation processes, however, do not appear to have been established.

♦ The findings suggest the following implications for the role of the LEA and the school in order for CPD to be successful, beneficial and purposeful:

> • All staff should have an input in to the School Development Plan to ensure that it reflects both the school's and individuals' needs, and so that all staff are striving towards the same goals.
>
> • The School Development Plan should inform the LEA's Education Development Plan.
>
> • CPD activities provided by the LEA should not only respond to national policies, but also to the needs identified in the schools' own SDPs and to the ongoing needs identified by CPD coordinators and/or headteachers.
>
> • Coordination between individual staff, the CPD coordinator and/or headteacher and the LEA advisory team is vital to secure appropriate and relevant CPD. An understanding of local needs and context by the LEA is fundamental to this process.
>
> • Evaluation forms, filled in following staff's participation in CPD (external), should be rigorous, systematic and viewed by the LEA advisory team to inform future CPD activities.

6. EFFECTIVE CPD

This chapter identifies and discusses the views of, and conditions that constitute, effective continuing professional development.

6.1 What is effective CPD?

This section will discuss perceptions of effective CPD, as revealed by the LEA and school questionnaires, and the case study interviews with staff.

6.1.1 LEA questionnaire

When asked to provide views about the most effective approaches to supporting the CPD needs of teachers to improve pupil achievement, a range of responses was given. All 105 LEAs responded to this open-ended question, providing a total of 239 responses. The most frequent response (56 responses) highlighted the importance of CPD activities that were directed and owned by teachers themselves:

> *Participants are not in receipt, i.e. do it **with** teachers not **to** teachers.*

Another important feature for ensuring the effectiveness of CPD provision was the use of collaborative approaches such as networking, mentoring, observations and teacher placements (46 responses).

Other examples of effective practice included: those that resulted from good communication and coordination (27 responses), for example teacher secondments to LEA advisory services, links with HEI, and effective local partnerships. Tailoring activities to schools' need (25 responses) was also felt to be a very effective approach.

Although cited as examples of effective approaches to CPD for raising achievement, the responses showed that nationally led CPD (11 responses) and CPD activities based on OFSTED information (six responses) were considered less effective than the more personal approaches described above. Working with schools and involving teachers directly when shaping the type of CPD provision on offer were generally viewed more favourably.

Key issues emerging from the questionnaires were that effective CPD activities need to:

- be clear and identify needs at both school and individual levels
- ensure that the timing of activities enables access
- include courses over a period of time

- allow time for courses to have an impact on teaching and learning

- take place in-school/classroom

- encompass a variety of approaches

- have the support of the headteacher and school network

- involve whole-school self-review

- share good practice

- encourage teachers to take on board what they need

- have follow-up courses in school

- provide a balance of theoretical underpinning and practical intervention.

These issues can be grouped into a number of themes:

- the identification of CPD needs (individual, school)

- the delivery of CPD (accessibility of venue, style and approach)

- the impact upon teaching and learning

- the role of the school (their approach, follow-up, support).

The LEAs provided information about what they considered to be effective CPD, but it was more difficult to establish which support strategies they employed (in response to this question). One LEA respondent, however, made explicit the implicit responses of many, by indicating that CPD activities were effective when the LEA:

- responded to stated needs

- tailor-made specific programmes for schools or consortia

- provided full and fair information

- kept schools informed about initiatives

- acted quickly

- operated a structured but flexible programme so that extra courses could be slotted in, in response to Government initiatives that occurred after planning the main programme.

These support issues imply that the role of the LEA should be to help identify CPD needs, and to respond with CPD activities that meet such needs, keeping up to date with requirements and initiatives.

6.1.2 School questionnaire

The final open-ended question in the school questionnaire asked respondents to identify the most effective strategies to support CPD to ensure that there was an impact on teaching and learning. Respondents tended to identify the nature of effective CPD rather than the strategy that supported it (see Table 6.1). However, the case study interviews invited staff to discuss how CPD was supported by the school and the LEA (see Chapter 7).

Table 6.1   Effective CPD by schools

CPD is effective when...	Frequency of mention
it is tailored (for individual teacher)	19
it is self-directed mentoring and observation	14
activities are targeted	13
it has a whole-school focus	12
the training/provider is high quality	11
it is linked with HEI	9
it has feedback and support	7
the timing is appropriate	5
funding is available	4
conferences/meetings are involved	4
it is ongoing	4
No response to this section	2
Total	108

Based on 42 schools. Respondents could give more than one response.

As can be seen, schools most commonly thought that CPD was effective when it was tailored to meet the needs of the teacher, when it was self-directed, and when activities were targeted. Respondents wrote that CPD activities should address the needs of the school and the individual, in terms of their personal and professional development. These issues have clear implications for the need identification processes (see Chapter 5).

The importance of a whole-school ethos, focusing upon whole-school development opportunities and the quality of the deliverer/delivery, were also frequent responses:

> *The development of the school as a centre for lifelong learning ... CPD is not just for teachers but for all staff, therefore creating an atmosphere of learning expectation.*

It was acknowledged that the nature of the activity and experience of teachers have an impact on the effectiveness of CPD activities. For example, one respondent suggested that the most effective approach for a newly qualified teacher was a good mentor and adequate discussion time.

Other respondents identified, to a lesser extent, that CPD activities need to:

- be properly funded, as funding on an annual cycle does not allow for the school to take a long-term strategic view.

- take place during the school day, and ideally on a training day, so that colleagues can work together.

- involve providers working with children, as this approach was considered to be more realistic and practically relevant than lecture-style CPD.

The core themes that emerged were that the most effective approaches to professional development activities were those which were:

- practical
- local
- classroom-based
- ongoing
- cost-effective
- in conducive surroundings
- led by a respected person with recent and relevant classroom practice.

As can be seen, these issues largely focus upon the delivery of the CPD: venue, style, and competence of deliverer. Similarly, findings emerged from a study by Lee (2000) in which teachers of varying length of service were asked in a survey, amongst other questions, what factors were seen to contribute to effective CPD. The research revealed that CPD needed to be relevant and realistic, and to provide opportunities to share ideas and good practice. CPD was also viewed as effective when it was hands-on, when there were sufficient resources, and when it was well delivered. Conversely, teachers suggested that CPD was ineffective when it had inappropriate or irrelevant content, and when it was poorly planned and badly focused.

6.1.3 Case study interviews with staff

Staff, with varying roles and responsibilities in schools, were asked their views about the characteristics of effective CPD, and to complete the phrase 'Effective CPD is when ...'. Table 6.2 reveals the nature and frequency of responses by primary, secondary and special school staff who were interviewed and who responded to the question. As can be seen, a wide array of responses was given, capturing issues which revolved around individual staff (professional, personal), the classroom (impact upon teaching and learning), the school (ethos, approach), the provider (deliverer, delivery), and other issues (time, resources, supply cover, support).

The most popular response (reported by 20 staff) related to the professional benefits of CPD, that is, when teaching skills were improved and when teachers became more confident and competent professionally. It was also mentioned, in this context, that CPD was effective when teachers wanted to keep up to date with developments and strove to improve their teaching skills:

> *Effective CPD is when teachers are empowered, self-confident so that they can deliver effectively and are involved in determining what it is.* (Secondary teacher)

> *CPD is effective when there is a willingness from staff to take part and rethink, re-evaluate practice and develop.* (Primary headteacher)

Table 6.2   Effective CPD, by staff within the three school types

Response categories		Details: Effective CPD is when...	Frequency of response by staff		
			Primary N = 41	Secondary N = 10	Special N = 9
Individual level	Professional	• there is a professional frame of mind • it makes for a better teacher • it improves practice/ teaching skills • teachers become more competent/confident • staff can keep up to date	13	3	4
	Personal	• there is a positive attitude • staff can strive to develop as individuals • CPD is chosen	9	1	3
Classroom level	Impact	• it impacts upon teaching and learning • it leads to improvements in the classroom • it benefits children	13	3	–
School level	Role of school	• there is a school ethos of professional development • there is a non-threatening, risk-taking environment	6	1	1
		• there is a whole-school approach • CPD is followed up	6	1	–
Provider level	Delivery	**Content:** • it is geared towards appropriate age group/ target group • it has clear aims/ objectives • it is interesting/ informative/up to date • it inspires ideas for teaching	9	2	3
		Tailored CPD: • it addresses/meets CPD needs (individual/ school/Government)	11	2	1
		Style: • it provides practical/ hands-on activities • it provides interactive learning	4	1	1
		Logistics: • it is at a convenient time • the venue is accessible • it sets up a good atmosphere	3	2	–
	Deliverer	• the deliverer has appropriate knowledge/ experience	1	–	–

(Table 6.2 continued on p. 57)

Table 6.2 *(continued)*

Response categories		Details: Effective CPD is when...	Frequency of response by staff		
			Primary N = 41	Secondary N = 10	Special N = 9
Other	Time	• there is appropriate release time	2	–	–
	Resources	• there are appropriate resources	2	–	–
	Supply cover	• there is adequate supply cover	2	–	–
	Support	• support is given	1	1	–

Also at the individual level, comments were made regarding the personal attitude and enthusiasm that was needed for CPD to be effective. Enthusiasm, interest and a deliberate choice to undertake CPD were seen as important characteristics. There was a perception that staff should want to better themselves and be committed to doing so.

CPD is effective when the person involved is committed and motivated (Special school teacher)

Overall, the second most popular view was that effective CPD was when it impacted upon teaching and learning in the classroom. Ultimately, this should result in improvements to children's learning. Staff often mentioned that this impact should be direct, and that visible changes in children's work, ability and behaviour should result. However, as one secondary teacher clearly expressed (see quotation below), the impact was often difficult to attribute directly to a particular CPD activity; it was more often an instinctive feeling that improvements had taken place (see also Chapter 8):

Effective CPD should have a direct and measurable impact on the pupils but very often has more of a 'feel' factor. Sometimes it can be measured, but sometimes you just feel that it has had an impact. (Secondary teacher)

Seeing changes in children's work and ability. (Primary teacher)

Overall, a high number of comments were made about the role of the provider. Staff reported that effective CPD depended upon the delivery of the training with regard to its content, whether it met the identified need, its style and the logistics. Details of teachers' views are given below.

Content: effective CPD is when the content is focused, challenging, informative and appropriate. Staff want to be able to see how they can use this new knowledge to inform their teaching; thus, it needs to be applicable to the appropriate key stage and/or target group:

It is effective when it doesn't waste time; when it is geared to the appropriate key stage. (Primary teacher)

Meeting need: effective CPD should be tailored to meet the training needs of the individual, school and Government priorities:

CPD is effective when it is tailored to individual needs. It needs to take account of people's experience, different backgrounds and prior knowledge. (Secondary teacher)

CPD is effective when it encompasses Government initiatives, the school, and individual pupil's needs. (Special school teacher)

Style: effective CPD is when there is a range of interactive delivery styles, activities and practical learning:

CPD is effective when there is variety, when it is interesting, when there is a range of activities on offer during the course, when time flies and when it is fun, e.g. ice breakers/silly games to put everyone in the mood. (Special school teacher)

Logistics: effective CPD is when the venue is accessible, the training is held at a convenient time, and staff are made to feel comfortable:

[CPD is effective when] it is at the right time (twilight teachers are less receptive) with some space to do it in, in a conductive atmosphere. (Primary teacher)

To a lesser extent, the school itself was reported as contributing to effective CPD through its ethos towards CPD, and its approach to identifying and following up training. Firstly, staff reported that CPD was effective when the school ethos encouraged professional development, providing opportunities for all staff, and where the school culture created a non-threatening environment where staff could try out different CPD activities and see what worked for them:

CPD is effective when it is a key feature within the school. CPD is as effective as the head makes it effective; when there is importance within the school culture. (Primary teacher)

Secondly, staff reported that CPD was effective when the school adopted a whole-school approach, where colleagues worked together to identify and address professional development needs (individual and common goals), and where activities were followed up within the school.

Finally, with reference to the other issues in Table 6.2, staff reported, to a lesser extent, that CPD was effective when there was adequate non-contact time, resources, support and supply cover.

6.2 Conditions for effective CPD

This section discusses the conditions that constitute effective CPD, as revealed by the case study interviews with LEA advisers and staff within the schools. This aimed to find out the factors that need to be in place, in order for CPD to be effective.

6.2.1 LEA findings

In the interviews, LEA advisers were asked which conditions they felt made for effective CPD. All three LEA advisers spoke of the importance of the school ethos and culture of professional development, where teachers were seen as learners and part of a lifelong learning organisation. One adviser felt that this emphasis upon a learning culture for all would be more likely to result in an impact upon teaching and learning. Another adviser spoke about the importance of team work, and that it was the role of the headteacher to encourage staff to work together as a team, and to be able to offer constructive criticism to one another. This climate of trust was seen as an essential condition for effective CPD within and between schools.

The LEA advisers indicated that their role was to work with schools, consulting with the CPD coordinator, and providing a variety of CPD activities that were appropriate. Other suggestions of initiatives that would create conditions for effective CPD were:

- Performance Management; this would help staff to develop and improve under guidance

- partnerships with higher education

- participation in Investors in People as a way of encouraging and sustaining professional development.

6.2.2 Staff findings

In the case study interviews, staff were asked which conditions they felt made for effective continuing professional development. The researcher suggested that such conditions might, for example, revolve around the personal or professional conditions that needed to be in place.

Staff of varying roles and responsibilities within the schools responded to this question. Responses can be grouped into conditions at four levels:

- individual level (personal, professional)

- school level (need identification, ethos)

- provider level (deliverer, delivery; logistics, content, style)

- LEA level

- other conditions that could potentially operate at various levels (time, resources, supply cover, linkages).

Table 6.3 reveals the frequency of responses by school type (primary, secondary, special school).

Table 6.3   Conditions for effective CPD by school type

Response Categories		Details	Frequency of response by school type		
			Primary N = 12	Secondary N = 3	Special N = 3
Individual level	Personal	• enthusiasm • commitment • desire to develop	10	3	3
Individual level	Professional	• improving practice/skills • wanting to make a difference • developing professionally/ promotion	4	3	2
School level	Role of school	• school ethos of professional development • climate where staff want to develop and are given opportunities • whole-school expectation	9	3	–
School level	Role of school	• school identifying need • selecting/providing relevant CPD that meets need • guiding staff development/support staff	6	2	3
Provider level	Deliverer	• appropriate knowledge/ experience/ background • enthusiastic and engaging • good presentation skills	7	1	2
Provider level	Delivery	**Content:** • clear aims • appropriateness/ applicability to age range/target group • ideas that can be implemented into teaching • interesting/ informative/ challenging • high quality	7	2	3
Provider level	Delivery	**Style:** • variety of format • practical activities • discussions/interactive	6	1	3
Provider level	Delivery	**Logistics:** • arrangements • practicalities • comfort	4	1	1
LEA level	Role of LEA	• approachable • provide support	2	–	–

(Table 6.3 continued on p. 61)

Table 6.3 *(continued)*

Response categories		Details: Effective CPD is when...	Frequency of response by school type		
			Primary N = 12	Secondary N = 3	Special N = 3
Other	Time	• time for CPD activity • time for consolidation • non-contact time	2	2	–
	Resources	• good resources • budget for CPD	4	2	1
	Supply cover	• money for supply cover • availability of supply	4	–	–
	Linkages	• linkages/close relationship with other schools	1	–	–

The findings are similar to the results reported in the previous section (effective CPD is when...), yet they provide more detail, as staff tended to discuss and evaluate their own CPD experiences. The suggested conditions, at the various levels, will now be discussed in turn.

Individual level

Staff in all school types most frequently mentioned the importance of the individual and his or her enthusiasm to participate in CPD. The individual's willingness and eagerness to better themselves were central to the personal conditions required for effective CPD. This may have been connected to personality, but nevertheless it was the motivation and commitment of the individual to want to improve.

Ideally, staff should have a choice as to their participation in CPD; they have got to want to do the activity. Numerous staff commented that if they were forced to participate in CPD then it would be ineffective. The DfEE CPD strategy (DfEE, 2001b) reported that funding for national strategies means that teachers' own development priorities are not always taken into account, and that teachers' access to and experience of professional development largely depends upon their school culture and circumstances (variability in resources and priorities). They indicate that one of the aims of the CPD strategy is to provide funding to allow teachers to choose and direct their own professional development. The NFER project findings certainly indicate that teachers' choice is an important aspect and condition for effective CPD:

> *Teachers need to perceive that there is a need, i.e. they have got to want to do it. If teachers are forced, it is not effective, there is resistance.* (Secondary teacher)

> *You've got to want to do the CPD. The school can send you and then you are not involved. So there needs to be a willingness to learn.* (Special school teacher)

Sometimes, personal circumstances, such as a young family, prevented teachers from wanting to participate, as they perceived that this commitment would involve personal compromises.

Professional motivations were also seen to contribute to effective CPD; staff wanted to become better teachers, to improve their practice, and ultimately to benefit the children. Once again, this drive had to come from within; staff must want to develop professionally and to improve their skills, in order for CPD to be effective:

> *Staff want to put their training needs forward because they want to be better teachers. Sometimes it is to develop new or additional responsibilities. They want to do it to feel more comfortable and reassured about what they are doing. The resistant staff feel they have 'been there and done that', and they have an insular view of teaching ... they have a lack of ambition for promotion.*
>
> (Secondary headteacher)

School level

The case studies revealed that the school facilitated effective CPD in two ways: through the ethos of professional development created within and throughout the school; and through the need identification processes used to select and/or provide relevant CPD. These issues will be addressed in turn.

In addition to comments reported earlier on the significance of the school ethos, other examples were given. It became apparent that this ethos was perceived to stem from the headteacher, reflecting his or her philosophy and enthusiasm for CPD. Staff reported that they saw headteachers as role models because they participated in professional development themselves, and encouraged it throughout the school.

One secondary headteacher stated:

> *Ethos of the school is important – it is seen as an efficient and effective learning environment and is part of lifelong learning. There is an expectation that teachers are learners too…. Professional development helps them to renew their growth continually.*

This view illustrates the importance placed upon teachers as learners, that headteachers want to invest in their staff. Furthermore, several headteachers mentioned that they recruited new staff who would become part of this culture:

> *When I interview new staff, I look at people who are willing to re-evaluate, take on new ideas, put into practice. The downside is that by giving them a useful course of PD they then get promotion so staffing becomes a problem, particularly in shortage areas.*
>
> (Primary headteacher)

One aspect of this ethos was the view that CPD was for development, rather than failure. Such non-threatening environments were further characterised by supportive colleagues and a trusting team environment.

Some teachers have felt threatened but there has been a change of philosophy and they are now willing to develop, whereas at one time teachers didn't want to change. (Primary CPD coordinator)

School ethos was important and in their school there was an expectation which resulted from their close-knit community and team work. (Primary teacher)

The role of the school in the need identification process was seen as a condition for effective CPD. It was reported that Performance Management would formalise this process. After the needs were identified, the school would either provide the training, or seek out relevant CPD activities.

Schools experienced difficulties in identifying appropriate CPD to meet their needs, as there was often no, or inaccurate, information about the course. Schools need clear and accurate information about courses so that they can make an informed choice:

I look at different providers and I am fairly choosy – there are so many training courses that it [CPD] *needs to be cost effective. Often there are problems in that the information accompanying a course is often not provided.* (Special school headteacher)

More often, the school provided its own CPD activities, as the best way of meeting its identified needs. Whole-school approaches were viewed as particularly important:

School provides CPD, and whole-school approaches are favoured as these meet need. They [staff] *valued training in school because it met their needs. Whole-school approaches enabled them to discuss it so they got feedback and were involved in discussion. This generated a consistency in approach.* (Primary headteacher)

Provider level

All school types reported that effective CPD depended upon conditions regarding the deliverer and the training delivery process: content, style, and logistics (see Table 6.3).

It was pointed out that deliverers must have an appropriate knowledge base and background. Thus, they must be competent and confident in the subject of their training. It was also reported that the deliverer must be enthusiastic and able to engage his/her audience.

In terms of the CPD delivery, three aspects of this process were mentioned: the content of the activity, the style of the delivery, and the logistics. CPD was deemed most effective when the content of the activity encompassed:

- clear aims, objectives and expectations

- appropriateness for applicability to the key stage or target group e.g. all special schools reported that the CPD should be specialised, focusing upon special needs issues, rather than including special needs as the afterthought

- information which is interesting, challenging and added something new

- sessions which are inspiring, useful, and could be practically implemented in the classroom.

In particular, several staff said that LEA courses were often effective as they were relevant, practical, applicable to teaching, and appropriate to their particular school and children:

> *LEA literacy updates are good as they are visual, clearly set out the objectives and are applicable to the classroom and there are not too many handouts.* (Primary teacher)

Comments on the delivery style were also fairly popular. Most often, staff talked about the importance of practical and interactive learning styles. These styles were viewed as most effective because they made the CPD more interesting and memorable:

> *Courses are best delivered when there is a combination of talking, providing an activity and feedback. Practical hands-on activities are favoured.* (Primary teacher)

> *There must be variety in their delivery, including practical involvement as more is learned via activities.* (Special school teacher)

Fewer schools mentioned the importance of the arrangements, practicalities and comfort. Those who did referred to the accessibility of the venue, seating arrangements, break times, and the overall comfort. All these components were seen to contribute to the overall enjoyment:

> *The venue is important: if there is a comfortable venue it helps teachers to feel valued and they go away thinking they've had a nice time.* (Primary headteacher)

> *It can often be difficult to switch off from school and be relaxed; courses need to recognise this by allowing a short while for tea/ coffee, and time to chat before starting the course.* (Primary teacher)

LEA level

Only two schools mentioned the role of the LEA and the value of an approachable and supportive advisory team. However, the role of the LEA in terms of course content and implications for accompanying course information has already been highlighted. LEA advisers who had a good relationship with a school were more likely to devise courses which met the specific needs of the school and thus were more effective.

Other conditions

Schools also referred to resources, supply cover, time and linkages. Mostly, schools reported that an adequate budget was essential in order for CPD to take place. One CPD coordinator spoke of the restrictions placed upon the funding streams which dictated the choice of activities. Adequate time to undertake and consolidate CPD was also mentioned; schools reported that appropriate non-contact time was essential to prepare for and implement CPD before momentum was lost. Furthermore, time was needed to prepare lessons in advance for the supply cover. Lack of supply cover, due to lack of resources or availability, had prevented several staff undertaking CPD. Some schools reported that they had used their supply money to recruit a full-time teacher; this increased non-contact time and CPD opportunities. Finally, one school reported that links with their feeder schools were essential for effective CPD.

6.3 Summary and implications for role of LEA

♦ This chapter has identified and discussed the views of, and conditions that constitute, effective CPD. A key finding was the importance of the school ethos that created an expectation that all staff participated in professional development activities, thus creating a learning culture for all. The headteacher, and a supportive team environment, were fundamental to encouraging whole-school opportunities and expectations. At an individual level, teachers felt that CPD was more effective when they were able to direct and choose their own professional development.

♦ CPD was viewed as effective when the deliverer was competent, and had appropriate background knowledge and expertise, and when the content was challenging, appropriate (to key stage) and up to date. With regard to delivery style, a varied style including practical demonstrations and discussions was favoured.

♦ Teachers considered CPD to be effective when it impacted upon teaching (skills and practice) and children's learning: practical and interactive activities were perceived most likely to facilitate this.

♦ Other requisites were: accessibility of venue, convenience, adequate non-contact time, resources, support and supply cover.

♦ The findings suggest that the LEA can facilitate and maximise the effectiveness of CPD by:

- **encouraging schools to raise the profile of CPD and to listen to their staff preferences so that they can identify and direct their own CPD**

- **providing detailed course information – objectives, expectations, target age and level**

- **liaising with schools, so that LEA courses meet their identified CPD needs; encouraging schools to involve all staff in developing their SDP**

- **devising CPD which offers new, challenging, up-to-date information which teachers can implement in the classroom**

- **appointing trainers who are competent, experienced, experts in their field**

- **favouring practical and interactive CPD, such as classroom demonstrations.**

7. SUPPORT STRATEGIES

Previous chapters have highlighted CPD activities undertaken by teachers, the procedures that are in place to enable them to participate and the conditions that contribute to the effectiveness of CPD. This section considers the role of the LEA and the school in supporting teachers' CPD.

The DfEE CPD strategy (DfEE, 2001b) highlights a number of organisations which have a key contribution to make to 'focused, practical development, especially where they establish continuing partnerships with schools and teachers'. The LEA is one such organisation.

Derrington (2000) points out that LEAs are required to offer educational services to schools and to provide performance data and focused support to schools on national priorities such as literacy, and to help spread best practice.

Larger authorities tended to provide support for all curriculum subjects. Smaller authorities were limited to providing support for the core subjects. Some LEAs concentrated professional development programmes on strategic EDP priorities rather than operating on a trading model. This was criticised by some as providing a fragmented service and failing to meet wide curriculum needs. However, questions were raised about the financial security for those offering full curriculum services and the viability for unpopular courses, which could be cancelled at short notice. This could lead to customer dissatisfaction and may effectively jeopardise future use of the service.

7.1 LEA strategies to support CPD activities

Chapters 4 and 5 show the role played by the LEA in supporting CPD activities. To explore the support strategies in place, interviewees were asked about their experiences of the support they had for CPD from the LEA. Case study school interviewees reported that the LEA provided training, advisory support, information, funding, partnerships and resources.

7.1.1 Training

All the case study schools identified the LEA as having a role in providing training, including in-school support, courses and conferences, and support for NQTs' induction year.

♦ **In-school support**

In-school support from the LEA was usually through the links that had been established with the adviser (see Chapter 4).

♦ **Courses and conferences**

The LEA provided courses and conferences for school staff. These were often subject orientated. In the primary schools, there was a focus on literacy and numeracy in response to the introduction of the National Literacy and Numeracy Strategies. There were also opportunities for subject coordinators to attend coordinator courses and for deputies to become involved in deputy headteacher conferences.

One secondary school suggested that courses were available in all subject areas, but in another school, a teacher felt that there was a shortage of opportunities in her subject area.

Special school interviewees indicated that courses and conferences were organised and provided by the LEA. One LEA provided a wide and varied programme of high quality, at a local destination which avoided the need for participants to travel great distances. However, in another LEA, courses were not used because they were too generic or because they did not focus on special educational needs.

♦ **NQT induction**

The LEA provided support for NQTs in primary and secondary schools during their induction year. This was not mentioned by interviewees in special schools.

7.1.2 Advisers and advisory team

In most cases, the work of advisers or advisory teams was the most highly appreciated because they provided training opportunities within the school and the LEA. They were mentioned in all school types, but headteachers, deputies professional development and subject coordinators, who had the most contact with advisers, provided the most detail. Examples have been given in Chapters 4 and 5.

7.1.3 Information

LEAs fulfilled their statutory duties by collecting and disseminating information. LEAs provided information about CPD opportunities in LEA-wide course booklets. In some LEAs, this was supplemented by flyers to remind participants and newsletters to keep subject coordinators up to date with initiatives. Some LEAs also provided details about courses on offer from other providers.

School staff said that the LEA was involved in establishing and encouraging local networks, subject and coordinator networks and discussion groups as well as facilitating links between schools. Advisers' knowledge about the local context enabled schools to disseminate their own good practice as well as to identify schools where they might go to observe good practice. The advisers' role was seen to be crucial in sharing knowledge across schools. Their local specialist knowledge contributed to successful and effective CPD. One example included establishing paired monitoring in the LEA. The LEA adviser had identified individual teachers in different schools who had similar needs and focus. She put them in touch so that they could support and monitor each other in the classroom.

In addition, one teacher in a special school received a support pack for her teacher/governor role from the LEA.

It was clear that advisers were most effective where there was a genuine consultation between schools and advisers, and in the role of a critical friend. As Chapter 5 showed, CPD needs were identified, negotiated and met by LEAs which enabled support over a period of time.

7.1.4 Funding

Headteachers were most likely to comment on funding as an aspect of the support offered by the LEA for CPD. Although they were appreciative of the funding available, they did not provide detailed information. In two LEAs, headteachers talked about the service level agreement that enabled them to choose from a range of CPD activities, as appropriate for their school. In another school, teachers mentioned that funding enabled them to participate in special projects or to undertake higher academic study.

In another primary school, where funding was decreasing this year, the headteacher had to look carefully at the LEA options available and to make difficult decisions about his CPD budget and provision for staff. A deputy headteacher felt that funding was a problem in a small LEA.

Staff in one secondary school, where the LEA had reduced in size considered that there had been a reduction in LEA support for CPD. Special school interviewees commented on the LEA role in funding CPD activities, including support for degree students.

Some headteachers said that delegated funding, which gave schools different options of buying services from the authority, had resulted in schools' looking closely at the quality of the provision before they made their choices. There was a feeling that there was less funding for activities than in previous years. One teacher commented that the lack of funding for supply cover detracted from the positive elements of participation in professional development activities. When supply teachers or funding were available, disruption to children's learning and extra pressure on other teachers were reduced. Another teacher was concerned that if enough schools did not buy into the LEA package, small schools would have problems in providing professional development activities for their staff.

7.1.5 Partnerships

One of the key issues identified by interviewees was the kinds of partnerships that existed between the school and the LEA. They recognised that the LEA provided a valuable link between Government initiatives and their implementation by schools. As one CPD coordinator commented, the LEA *'interprets the whims of the Government into something more manageable'*. This was endorsed by staff in a special school.

Another headteacher felt that the partnership between the LEA and school was particularly beneficial because the adviser provided in-school support and enabled the school to share its good practice with other schools.

The personal element of the adviser–school partnership was important and CPD was most effective when the advisers were consistent, credible and able to bridge the gap between the demands of the LEA EDP and the school SDP.

A deputy headteacher felt that his involvement with the LEA made him feel part of a bigger team, which gave him a wider view of the education system.

Partnerships between schools, LEA and HEIs had been established. In one case, the LEA had a facilitating role. An interviewee commented that at one stage there seemed to have been an equal partnership, based on funding and delivery of the teaching, but now the HEI seemed to be taking on the LEA role in providing activities.

One special school interviewee described the LEA role as a facilitator for CPD activities. In contrast, another special school interviewee commented that because advisers were cheaper than consultants, the school only used consultants when there were no other options.

7.1.6 Shared resources

A number of deputies, coordinators and teachers reported that the LEA provided access to resources. This support strategy had a direct impact on teachers' professional development and classroom practice. The resources available included:

- access to a series of long-, medium- and short-term lesson plans: although useful in their present form, the coordinator was looking forward to being able to access them on a CD so that she could make adjustments to fit the school's needs

- materials for schools with a lack of appropriate resources

- opportunities for schools to take children to the professional development centre, to work with an adult as part of a wider LEA training package

- the LEA internet site

- booklets about aspects of teaching

- resources which teachers could borrow.

7.1.7 Other support provided by the LEA

LEA support strategies identified by schools and teachers included:

- a technician to help with the production of a video for training purposes

- support for governors
- a variety of activities offered to schools
- up-to-date information
- internet access.

Most of the interviewees in the case study schools identified the strategies in place in the LEA to support their professional development but also highlighted where they felt improvement could be made. The most frequently mentioned areas referred to the quality of advisers and of courses.

7.1.8 Quality of advisers

Several schools reported that if the advisers were good, the school would buy into the LEA provision. Schools were generally willing to use the adviser's local knowledge and, in most cases, positive relationships between advisers and schools had been established. Many interviewees, especially in small authorities, felt that they knew their advisers and were able to contact them easily. One school reported that this relationship helped to balance the support and threat element of the annual review. One teacher commented that she did not really enjoy being observed by the adviser but the feedback helped to identify an action plan to develop her practice, which made her feel more confident.

Another school questioned the quality of the adviser in terms of consistency and credibility of advice. One school challenged the credibility of an adviser whose written feedback talked about Year 2 children in a school whose intake started with Year 3. In another school, although the adviser provided continuity and consistency, the headteacher felt that one person did not always have credibility in all subject areas.

7.1.9 Quality of courses

Primary school interviewees commented on the variability in the quality of courses and said that schools were becoming more selective in picking out appropriate elements. As one headteacher explained, 'we cherry-pick the courses and conferences we want'. Other primary schools were critical of the course details, which did not always match what was provided, and, in those cases, the participants felt that funding had been misspent and time had not been well used. Where advertising outlined clear course objectives, which were met in the course, teachers participating were satisfied.

Two primary teachers criticised courses comprising group discussion and plenary feedback, as this did not take forward their professional development in the classroom.

7.1.10 Other challenges

Overall, school staff were very aware of the support they received from their LEA. Only two primary headteachers had very little to say about the LEA support for their staff CPD. One headteacher felt that she organised much of the professional development in her school herself, because she had previously been involved as a CPD adviser in another authority. The other headteacher realised that her school now had less support, because it was LEA policy to support weak schools and her school no longer fell into that category.

Other comments from primary headteachers focused on the gaps that emerged when professional development activities did not link the LEA EDP and the school SDP. Advisers were a vital link in that they knew the school, but often schools developed priorities, unaware of the LEA EDP identified priorities. LEA and school priorities were not always compatible. There was a need for flexibility so that school needs were met. In one LEA, the interviewees wanted time to consolidate the outcomes of one LEA initiative before having to move on to the next.

Secondary school staff were less likely than primary school staff to comment about the support from the LEA. In two secondary schools, most of the support was considered to come from within the school.

Five interviewees felt that the LEA did not have much of a presence in their professional development, offering neither financial nor practical help. Five others stated that the LEA was less supportive following reorganisation into a smaller LEA. Consequently they felt that the role of the LEA had changed from providing CPD activities to supporting school CPD activities by generating lists of experts and opportunities. In the scaling down, the LEA had become 'lean and mean' and headteachers felt that the existing informal networks within the LEA were stronger than the support offered by the authority.

Special schools appreciated the advisers or advisory teams when they were accessible, when they responded to requests quickly, and when they knew the school and the children so that they provided appropriate resources and courses. Even if they did not have the expertise themselves, advisers were available to help plan and organise an appropriate activity for the school. However, some interviewees felt that advisory support was not always as good as it could be, especially when they did not know who to contact, and when the quality of advisers' CPD provision varied. Where advisers were good, they were used by schools; if schools were dissatisfied with the quality of provision, they tended to look elsewhere. Advisers had a role in listening to and being in tune with school needs, so that they were able to provide appropriate courses in the future.

In one LEA special school, staff commented that they did not always feel supported by the LEA because the courses provided were not specialised enough to meet their needs; but in another LEA, this had been overcome by the advisers helping to arrange more specialist support and training.

7.2 Support strategies from the school

Interviewees mentioned a range of support strategies in place in school for their professional development.

7.2.1 Primary schools

Interviewees in primary schools felt that the school was very supportive of their professional development. Only one teacher thought that school support was limited. The responses of interviewees are indicated in Table 7.1. They could identify more than one strategy.

Table 7.1   Support strategies identified by primary school staff

Support strategy	Frequency of response
School staff	34
Attitude, ethos, culture, expectations within the school	16
Monitoring	14
Time allocated	13
Teamwork	11
Funding	11
Staff meetings	9
Total	108

The most frequently cited response was linked to school staff who supported CPD. (See Table 7.2). It was through them that teachers derived support from the attitude, ethos, culture and expectations developed within the school. Other strategies identified also stemmed from the commitment of these school staff. The commitment of headteachers to developing their staff was reflected by organising time for teachers to do things and encouraging teamwork throughout the school (see Chapter 5).

Table 7.2   Staff in primary schools supporting teachers' CPD

Primary school personnel	Frequency of response
Headteacher	9
Subject coordinator	9
Other staff	6
SMT	4
CPD coordinator	4
Governors	2
Total	34

As Chapters 5 and 6 show, the culture created by the headteacher and expectation of CPD in the school supported teachers' professional development.

Monitoring was another support strategy used in primary schools. This was appreciated in that it allowed teachers to identify their own professional needs and also aided identification of weaknesses in children's learning, which might then be addressed through the teachers' professional development.

Monitoring procedures included:
- auditing provision
- discussing teaching
- tracking children's progress
- identifying teachers' CPD needs
- documenting professional development progress, through evaluation forms (see Chapter 5).

Time allocation: Teachers appreciated the time made available for them to undertake professional development activities. For one, this was day release with supply cover; for others, it involved releasing the subject coordinator to provide support. In one school, the deputy had a 'floating' role so she was able to provide cover when teachers focused on professional development. In other schools, the headteacher covered classes because of the lack of available funding or availability of supply teachers. One teacher appreciated the flexibility in her school, which meant that when meetings clashed with her CPD or other events, meetings were changed so that she could complete the CPD activity after school and also take part in the meeting. Teachers also commented that there was a need to include planning time for CPD and to allow time for the CPD to make an impact or have an effect.

Teamwork: A number of interviewees felt the teamwork within the school enhanced, supported and facilitated their professional development. For some, it was the opportunity to have a professional dialogue with colleagues; for others, it involved planning in supportive year group teams.

Staff meetings: Many staff meetings were used for professional development, mainly to disseminate information and ideas gained from external CPD activities. Interviewees commented on the quality of the dissemination, indicating that it reflected the ability of the member of staff reporting back as well as the quality of the activity (see Chapter 4).

Tensions sometimes arose in primary schools where teachers shared their expertise within the school and in other schools. It was noted that while teachers were providing demonstration lessons, the learning of their own class was disrupted. In one school, parents were displeased with the impact it might have on their children.

7.2.2 Secondary schools

Lack of time prevented one headteacher from being asked about support strategies within the school. All other interviewees mentioned at least one strategy (see Table 7.3). One teacher commented that the very fact of being out of the classroom gave teachers a break from the children. However, this absence also interrupted the continuity and security of the class, which could have a negative effect, especially on difficult children. Because this teacher did not want this negative spiral to happen in his class, he did not undertake many CPD activities.

Table 7.3 Support strategies identified by secondary school staff

Suppoprt strategy	Frequency of response
School staff	14
School system/structures	5
Time allocated/staff meetings	5
Funding	2
Appraisal/performance management	2
Providing information	2
Other – developmental points, NQT induction	12
Total	32

School staff were the most frequently mentioned support strategy in secondary schools. The CPD coordinator was mentioned by eight teachers. In all three case study schools, coordinators were part of the senior management team. CPD coordinators were perceived to be the people with whom to discuss CPD needs and as the gatekeepers for participation in a CPD activity.

Allied to the CPD role, coordinators had systems to support other staff in identifying appropriate activities and evaluating their impact on teaching (see Chapter 5).

As in primary schools, secondary school respondents also mentioned the high profile of professional development and an expectation that it was part of the teaching package. Colleagues, including headteachers, were said to support professional development, and the allocation of time enabled participants to complete CPD activities.

Only two interviewees commented on funding. One headteacher highlighted the school's contribution to IQEA (see Appendix A4.4), and one teacher was aware that she had been unable to undertake an activity because of financial limitations.

Appraisal and performance management were said to be supportive by two interviewees, but they did not provide further details. Two other interviewees appreciated that the school provided information about CPD activities.

One teacher showed how the creation of career development points within the school supported his professional development. He explained that:

> *as part of the school improvement plan, career development posts had been created. Each year the governors funded a number of career development points to give all staff the opportunity to work on an area for a limited time (one or two years). It gave members of staff the opportunity to have a whole-school viewpoint and presented them with new challenges. It was effective because it was a temporary challenge which allowed for personal flexibility and gave staff an opportunity to decide if it was where their career should progress. Sometimes, it led to retention difficulties as staff had enhanced their curriculum vitae and were able to move on.*

In another secondary school, the LEA and an HEI supported the induction year but the school had made adjustments to improve the provision for the NQT in their school. In the school there was:

> *the view that NQTs and initial teacher training students brought in an attitude that professional development was about developing people. NQTs had ten per cent release time. This worked out at almost three periods of release time each week throughout the year. The CPD coordinator considered this was a fragmented use of time and that it was equivalent to six days' release in a block. The NQTs were allocated supply cover for six days, which enabled them to develop a block programme of shadowing within the school, visiting other schools as well as time to develop their ideas.*

7.2.3 Special schools

In special schools, one headteacher, a teacher and a special needs support assistant were not asked about the strategies in place in school to support professional development. Three special school staff said that they felt supported for their CPD activities by the school but did not provide tangible examples. Table 7.4 shows the responses.

Table 7.4   Support strategies identified by the special school staff

Suppoprt strategy	Frequency of response
School staff	6
Funding including supply cover	5
Time allocated	5
Ethos within the school	3
Information	2
Systems in place	2
Total	23

As with the primary and secondary schools, the school staff were cited as support strategies for CPD activities. The CPD coordinator was specifically mentioned by two teachers.

Funding was mentioned by five school staff: a headteacher, two CPD coordinators and two LSAs. The LSAs were appreciative of the funding made available by the school for whole-school professional development. It included paying LSAs to attend some of the closure days.

7.3 Summary

- It was clear that all types of school had strategies in place to support CPD activities, both from the LEA and within the school.

- The LEA provided and facilitated training through in-school support, courses and conferences, and NQT induction. The advisers and advisory terms were central in the LEA support strategy and contributed through a range of activities. Another support strategy focused on collecting and disseminating information about CPD activities and in establishing links to develop networks.

- Some LEAs offered support through funding and established service level agreements. Concerns were raised where funding had been, or was about to be, decreased.

- Schools valued the partnerships they had with the LEA and shared resources.

- The quality of the advisers working with the schools was important and was reflected by the schools' uptake of LEA provision.

- In all types of schools, support strategies for CPD centred around the ethos and culture of the school. This played an important part in effective CPD and was reflected in the role adopted by school staff. The CPD coordinator had a key role to play. Allocation of time and funding support also contributed to professional development.

8. IMPACT OF CPD ACTIVITIES ON TEACHING AND LEARNING

The CPD strategy (DfEE, 2001b) suggests that teachers should be selecting CPD activities that will have an impact on their teaching. Little is said about the kind of impact that could be expected or how it might be evaluated. MORI (1995) found that little was known about the 'nature and extent of CPD activity let alone the evidence of its efforts'. Flecknoe (2000) and Keating (2001) identify difficulties in judging the impact of professional development activities, other than at an easily measurable level.

This NFER project attempted to discover whether CPD activities had an impact on teaching and learning and, if so, how teachers measured any impact on children's learning.

8.1 Evaluation of impact

The questionnaire for the LEA survey included two references to the impact of CPD activities, though respondents were not specifically asked about this. One LEA respondent was keen to point out that

> *however good the provision, it is how the school makes sense of it in a considered, coordinated way which makes the difference in terms of effectiveness*

and another wrote

> *how, when and where CPD is delivered is less important than its effectiveness in terms of pupils' learning and quality of teaching.*

Other respondents commented on the cyclical nature of CPD activities. It was important for CPD to have an impact on teaching and learning as part of the cycle. One respondent explained that there was a need to ensure that action plans and targets for improving practice were put in place as a result of CPD.

Another respondent highlighted that any impact should be reflected in raised standards in the quality of teaching and learning.

8.1.1 School views

In the school survey, respondents were asked about the methods used to evaluate the impact of CPD activities on teaching and learning. In some schools, there was an expectation that the CPD activity should or could have an impact on teaching and learning. Table 8.1 shows how the impact of CPD activities was evaluated.

Table 8.1   Evaluating the impact of CPD activities

Method used	Frequency of response
Classroom observation	38
Reviewing school targets	37
Comparing performance data	36
Assessing changes in lesson planning	32
Other	15
Total	158

Based on 42 schools. Respondents could give more than one response.

Respondents who identified other methods of evaluating the impact of CPD activities provided examples which included:

- interviewing pupils or completing questionnaires about teaching and learning to identify children's perceptions of how they learn

- using children's work in books as evidence of impact on teaching and learning

- researching into classroom-based practice, for example investigating the effects of inclusion

- identifying good practice.

Respondents who cited classroom observations went on to refer to the impact of the CPD activity on the quality of teaching and learning in the classroom. One respondent wrote that it might be reflected in '*pupil participation/ enjoyment/ engagement/improved behaviour and concentration.*'

Action research was identified as having an impact. One respondent explained that this was because '*we look at, share and reflect on changes and how they impact on teaching and learning*'.

8.1.2 Case study schools

To explore some of the ideas presented in the surveys, all but three interviewees in the case study schools were asked about the impact of CPD activities on their teaching and children's learning.

Interviewees identified ways in which they thought their professional development had an impact on their teaching, but found it more difficult to comment on the effect they thought it had on children's learning. Many interviewees assumed that any effect on their teaching would have an impact on children's learning. Teaching and learning were perceived to be interlinked, but for ease of analysis they have been separated in this section.

8.2 Impact on teaching

Interviewees' immediate response when asked whether their professional development activity had an impact on their teaching varied from '*I hope so*' to '*yes, loads*' or '*yes, an astonishing effect*' and in most cases they were able to give examples that supported their claim. This supports the MORI survey (MORI, 1995). Headteachers tended to talk about whole-school impact, while classroom teachers tended to give details about any impact on them and in the classroom.

8.2.1 Headteachers' views on impact of CPD activities on teaching throughout the school

Headteachers were all committed to the professional development of their teachers.

You don't get school improvement by working hard. You get it through better teaching and effective learning. Professional development is bound to have an impact. (Secondary headteacher)

Other primary headteachers were more cautious, and one suggested that improvement was not '*just about CPD, but attitude, subject coordinators' leadership and teachers' personal willingness to take ideas on board*'.

Another primary headteacher was aware that not all professional development had an impact. It was her view that the impact varied according to the quality of the CPD experience. Another primary headteacher pointed out that some CPD activities had been undertaken too recently to see any impact on teaching and learning, and another felt that there had been an impact but could not say what it was.

Keating (2001) identified teachers' increased confidence as a result of completing a course. This view was supported by the NFER study, in which headteachers remarked that professional development in their school had led to more confident teachers who were more informed about their specialism. Teachers had increased awareness of what made them more effective as well as being more positive role models for children. More specifically, headteachers commented on a change in teaching attitude and climate within the school and a greater range of teaching styles and strategies being utilised.

In primary schools, the changes were identified as leading to

- a more 'open door' approach throughout the school. Teachers were less anxious about being observed by colleagues and were therefore more likely to share ideas and to welcome each other into their classrooms

- greater consistency and continuity throughout the school

- a more structured and focused teaching style with more thorough planning and assessment

- greater awareness of children's learning

- enhanced displays

- closer liaison with other schools

- improved documentation, such as lesson planning and record-keeping by subject coordinators.

In one secondary school, teachers were (said to be) more prepared to take risks in trying out new ideas and different teaching styles and were more confident to talk about their practice. Another headteacher was aware that (because the majority of the staff had been involved in a CPD activity) there was now greater consistency in teachers' expectations of pupils throughout the school.

Special school headteachers identified greater confidence in their teachers, stemming from CPD activities which had enabled teachers to deal with the children's increasingly complex needs.

The second change was a greater range of teaching styles. In both primary and secondary schools, headteachers felt that the CPD activities their staff had undertaken had led to a greater range of teaching styles being used and different strategies developed to enhance the teaching in the schools. Primary headteachers who felt that there had been an impact identified that:

- children were regrouped and were now working in a more collaborative way in the classroom

- there was a greater focus on practical work in the classroom

- lesson structures were adapted so that there was now more pace

- different schemes and resources had been established throughout the schools.

One secondary headteacher felt that teachers were using more teaching strategies, but did not elaborate. Special school headteachers did not identify this as part of the impact of CPD in their schools.

8.2.2 Teachers' views about the impact of CPD activities on their teaching

From the interview data, it was possible to group responses into different categories. Table 8.2 shows the range and frequency of responses in the case study schools and from the interviewees.

Table 8.2   Impact of CPD activities on teaching

Impact identified	Primary		Secondary		Special	
	No. of schools	Interviewees identifying the impact	No. of schools	Interviewees identifying the impact	No. of schools	Interviewees identifying the impact
Individual teachers						
Greater range of teaching styles	11	15	3	7	2	2
Enhanced confidence	8	11	3	4	2	2
Changes in resources	6	8	3	3	3	2
A more practical focus in implementation of ideas	7	9	2	4	1	1
Planning and assessment improved	7	8	0	0	2	2
Personal growth	7	8	1	2	1	3
Whole school						
Culture change in school	1	1	1	1	1	1
Improved documentation	1	1	1	1	1	1
Whole-school projects	1	2	0	0	1	1
Linked projects	1	1	0	0	1	1
Greater enthusiasm	1	1	1	1	0	–
Change in organisation	1	1	0	0	0	–

As Table 8.2 shows, teachers' views were similar to those expressed by headteachers. The most frequently cited impact in all three phases was related to changes in teaching style. For some, this included a greater variety of style being adopted and for others, it meant adopting a different approach for different activities. Some teachers became facilitators, so that children had greater control over their learning; others became more structured, with detailed and focused planning and clearer assessment.

Primary schools identified shorter lessons with greater pace and more collaborative work for children.

The development of teachers' confidence was considered to be another impact that professional development was having across the phases. In primary schools, teachers felt more able to share ideas with other staff and to implement changes in organisation in the classroom and in the school.

Secondary schools identified that teachers' greater confidence led to the ability to take part in professional discussion and allowed them to adopt different teaching styles.

In special schools, the increased confidence led interviewees to be more analytical in their approach to teaching and so they were able to extend the opportunities available for children. As one coordinator explained, her role in providing INSET for the staff had developed her confidence in working as part of a team, had given her an extended vocabulary, and had enabled her to develop resources to use with the staff and children and to contribute to changing the expectations and culture of the school.

Details of the other areas of impact identified in the case study interviews are listed below.

Development of resources

This was particularly the case in the primary schools, which had been involved in literacy and numeracy. As a result of literacy and numeracy training, primary teachers said they were now using:
*   big books
*   games
*   mental maths
*   a different reading scheme
*   a new handwriting approach.

Practical impact in the classroom

Linked to changes in, and development of, resources, teachers found practical elements of professional activities particularly useful, especially when they were able to use the ideas in the classroom with immediate effect. Primary school teachers provided the most examples of where they had found the practical elements of their professional development useful. For example, one teacher, who attended a practical art course that focused on techniques adopted by famous painters, used those techniques with her class to produce skilful reproductions of well-known paintings.

Planning and assessment

In primary schools, planning and assessment were said to have improved by becoming more structured, with clearer learning objectives. Assessment was more focused in primary and special schools.

Personal growth

Areas of personal development were also considered to have been strengthened by CPD activities in some schools of all types. Interviewees said that they were now able to identify their own strengths and weaknesses more easily, and that they had changed their attitude towards teaching and adopted a new outlook, as well as developing their own skills. For one, this was reflected in adopting an action research approach to her teaching.

Teachers recognised that it was easier to identify the impact of their professional development activities on teaching when these addressed visual or skill-based issues. The art activity described is one such example. Enhanced computer skills were also easily demonstrated.

Primary and special school teachers identified the impact on the whole school more readily than secondary school teachers. The literacy coordinator in one primary school commented that liaison with other schools had an impact on her work because it enabled her to be inspired by ideas and see a different approach. It also gave her confidence and an opportunity for professional dialogue, which resulted in increased enthusiasm. For some teachers, changes in the school ethos and culture were attributed to professional development activities. In other schools, improved documentation, changes in organisation and involvement in whole-school projects occurred after teachers' participation in professional development activities.

8.2.3 Monitoring the impact of CPD activities on teaching

Headteachers and CPD coordinators were asked whether the impact of CPD activities had been monitored. Most interviewees said that this was done informally, but others identified monitoring through:

- the work of the CPD coordinator, who kept track of CPD activities

- monitoring by subject leaders/coordinators and heads of department

- processes which were part of a larger CPD project

- tracking children. For example, in one primary school, teachers' participation in the National Literacy Strategy activities led to the development of a pupil tracking sheet. This demonstrated that previous areas of weaknesses identified in children's learning had been addressed by teachers attending National Literacy Strategy training activities provided by the LEA and the language coordinator in the school.

- professional development evaluation forms, which not only kept track of individual teachers' profiles, but also enabled the CPD coordinator to evaluate the impact within the school after completion of the professional development activity (see Chapter 5)

- reports to governors, which were based on observation in school.

8.3 Impact of CPD activities on children's learning

Even though interviewees found it more difficult to identify the impact on children's learning than the impact on their teaching, they still felt that there was one. Headteachers identified a whole-school perspective, and teachers tended to focus on the children in their own classroom.

8.3.1 Headteachers' views on the impact of CPD on children's learning

Nine of the 12 primary headteachers commented on the impact teachers' CPD activities had on children's learning throughout the school. They were cautious about making strong claims because they felt that there were other contributing factors. However, two primary headteachers felt confident that the impact could be seen in:

- children's work, which demonstrated greater knowledge and understanding

- the quality of the displays in the classroom

- the ability of children to talk more confidently and knowledgeably about their work.

Another three primary headteachers suggested that children's National Curriculum levels were improving in their school. One attributed this to teachers' greater confidence in awarding level 3 in science. Another headteacher pointed out that it felt as though children had improved, but that it was too soon to see an effect on the National Curriculum assessment scores, and improvement was difficult to pinpoint in areas that were not assessed.

Other comments referred to evidence of children's increased computer competence, raised self-esteem and greater awareness of what they were learning and their own progress.

Two secondary headteachers expected CPD activities to have an effect on children's achievements. One expressed similar sentiments to those of the primary headteachers, and suggested that it was difficult to pinpoint the effect on children's learning. He felt, however, that the ethos at the school and the expectation that teachers undertake professional development activities contributed to their increasingly successful examination levels.

Two special school headteachers suggested that the staff professional development was reflected in children's increased assessment levels, higher self-esteem and, in one school, a more enthusiastic and patient approach in the classroom.

8.3.2 Teachers' views about the impact of CPD activities on children's learning

Teachers were asked whether they thought their professional development activities were having an impact on children's learning. Most interviewees felt that there was an effect but found it difficult to give specific examples or tangible evidence. One or two teachers felt that it was too early for some activities to have had an impact on children's learning. They would expect to see improvements in children's work or a more positive attitude and response in lessons by the following year.

One special school teacher explained that any impact on children's learning was difficult to judge in special education. However, six interviewees in special schools felt that their professional development did have an impact (see Table 8.3).

Several interviewees indicated that they would monitor the impact through observations in the classroom, informal tests, external tests and the LEA annual review of children's attitude and their work. These approaches were similar to those identified by teachers who had already noted an impact on children's learning.

Table 8.3   Impact of CPD activities on teaching

Impact demonstrated by	Primary		Secondary		Special	
	School	Teacher	School	Teacher	School	Teacher
Improved achievement/ grades/National Curriculum levels	6	8	2	4	2	3
Greater enjoyment, enthusiasm towards school and work	6	9	2	3	2	3
Social impact, i.e. more collaboratively work and better communication with each other	3	3	0	0	1	2
Raised self-esteem	3	3	0	0	0	0
Ability to talk about ideas in greater depth	2	2	1	1	0	0
Earlier identification of SEN by teachers	1	1	0	0	0	0

For a range of teachers, evidence of their increased professionalism was reflected in children's learning. They felt that because of their participation in various professional development activities, children were performing better and achieving higher National Curriculum levels and examination grades and they were also more enthusiastic, engrossed and engaged in their learning. They were more positive towards their work, had a sense of accomplishment and raised self-esteem.

The most direct impact was seen by one secondary head of department who, having completed a CPD activity, introduced new styles of note-taking, which were well received by pupils.

8.4 Summary

♦   It was clear that it was difficult for teachers to make a direct link between the professional activity and any impact on teaching and learning. Tangible evidence was not always readily available, but there was a belief, by both headteachers and the rest of the staff, that professional development activities were having an impact on teaching and children's learning. One secondary teacher suggested that a high profile for CPD activity had an impact on attracting new staff to the school and raised the school profile throughout the LEA.

  •   There was an assumption/expectation that CPD will have an impact in school, on teachers, in the classroom and on children's learning.

  •   It was easier for teachers to identify impact on teaching than on learning.

  •   CPD led to increased confidence for teachers.

  •   Monitoring the impact of CPD is usually informal, although some interviewees identified more systematic procedures.

  •   Impact was felt at a school and individual level.

  •   Determining a direct link between CPD and impact was difficult as tangible evidence was not always readily available.

♦   The LEA was not mentioned in this section of the interview. It may be that the LEA could help school staff identify ways to monitor and establish evidence of impact on teaching and learning.

9. FUTURE CPD

It is evident that teachers' professional development is a key issue in the Government's future plans. The CPD strategy (DfEE, 2001b) highlights existing practice and identifies ways forward through increased funding, encouraging schools to become professional learning communities, introducing two new initiatives and encouraging teachers to open Individual Learning Accounts. In support of this focus, the General Teaching Council (GTC) also outlined its advice for CPD.

Interviews in case study schools in this research gave teachers the opportunity to suggest the way forward for CPD. They were asked what kinds of CPD activities should be developed in the future so that there was an impact on children's learning. Teachers' suggestions related mainly to:

♦ the type of activity

♦ the time required

♦ the nature of the activity.

Other issues were identified by only a few teachers in any one phase.

9.1 Types of activity

Interviewees felt that future CPD activities should be available both within the school and external to the school.

9.1.1 Activities within the school

Table 9.1 shows the kinds of activities which staff felt could be held in school.

Table 9.1   Types of activities identified within the school

Internal CPD activities	Primary staff	Secondary staff	Special staff
Teamwork development	6	8	3
Greater whole-school, subject/ specialist focus	8	1	3
Practical suggestions	2	1	5
ICT training	4	1	1
Up-to-date information	0	0	4
Outside speakers in school	2	1	0
Demonstration lesson	8	0	0
More work with children	0	2	0
Total	30	14	16

In all phases, interviewees indicated that future opportunities for activities should involve teamwork, have a whole-school approach, have a subject/specialist focus, be practical and include ICT.

Teamwork in primary schools would involve the subject coordinator more and share good practice within school. For one teacher, it would include attending a CPD activity with colleagues, so that ideas could be discussed and shared. In the secondary phase, the focus tended to be on team building at departmental level and working within and across departments to develop ideas, not just cascading information.

In special schools, future activities to develop teamwork would include working with other agencies, as well as sharing ideas/resources with their own staff.

There was a demand for greater whole-school focus or subject/specialist focus. Primary teachers referred to Government initiatives and monitoring and developing of subject areas. Secondary teachers wanted more subject-related activities and opportunities to develop resources and write schemes. Special school interviewees wanted more specialist activities to cater for teachers working with children with special educational needs.

CPD should provide practical suggestions which could be readily implemented. A few interviewees in all phases mentioned ICT but gave no details; however, one special school interviewee identified the use of the internet.

Demonstration lessons were already a significant part of CPD activities available in primary schools; only staff in this phase mentioned that they should be continued as part of CPD.

Inviting outside speakers to the school was identified as a possible future strategy in primary and secondary schools. Four special school interviewees felt that special education was changing so rapidly that up-to-date information would be an important element in future CPD development.

9.1.2 External CPD activities

Interviewees also identified activities that should be available external to the school environment. Table 9.2 overleaf shows the responses.

Primary school staff, in particular, saw opportunities to work with other schools and to visit other schools, especially when children were in school, as a valuable form of professional development.

Table 9.2   Future CPD activities outside the school environment suggested by interviewees

Extended CPD activities	Primary staff	Secondary staff	Special staff
Visits to other schools and observation in the practical environment	18	3	0
Opportunities for research, further study and involvement with HEIs	4	1	3
Conferences, outside speakers and 'away days'	5	0	0
Continuation/development of existing projects	2	1	0
Total	29	5	3

9.2   Time required

As mentioned in previous chapters, many teachers felt that there was insufficient time for professional development, and posed four possible solutions (see Table 9.3).

Table 9.3   Interviewees' views about availability of time for CPD

Time should be made available through:	Primary staff	Secondary staff	Special staff
secondment	8	3	2
more training days	4	3	1
more regular integrated non-contact time including use of floating staff	6	1	1
closure days at the beginning and end of term	0	1	0
Total	18	8	4

Secondment was mentioned by interviewees in all phases, in connection with national and international opportunities and teacher exchanges. One primary teacher suggested that a half-term secondment would be more effective in her teaching than the half-a-day-a-week model.

Interviewees in all phases favoured more training days and regular non-contact time. Two primary headteachers suggested that the number of closure days should be doubled, although this would have implications for teachers' pay and conditions of service. Secondary school interviewees suggested that they would like more training days, and went on to suggest that these would be useful for team building and working together on departmental rather than school issues. In the special schools, only one headteacher wanted an increase in training days and greater choice about how they were used.

Six primary interviewees suggested more regular and integrated non-contact time to develop their coordinator role and subject expertise. Most realised that releasing teachers would require a floating teacher.

One primary school deputy suggested that, instead of teaching for five full days, teachers should receive a half-day release per week to compensate for attendance at CPD in twilight sessions. This would make twilight sessions more acceptable.

Another primary headteacher suggested that better use could be made of a block of time, rather than short periods of time over several weeks. This was echoed by a teacher in a different primary school who favoured planned, longer training opportunities every few years, for example ten days rather than the present half-day arrangements. Another primary headteacher thought that the label 'non-contact' time was inappropriate and should be renamed 'management' time.

One secondary teacher drew on the Australian model where professional development takes place in a block of time at the beginning and end of each term. This enables departments to work together cohesively.

Table 9.4 presents the comments of interviewees with regard to length and timing of CPD activities.

Table 9.4   Interviewee comments about the length and timing of CPD activities

Time needed:	Primary staff	Secondary staff	Special staff
to implement/consolidate/ reflect on new initiatives and ideas and develop resources	7	5	6
for longer courses	2	2	0
for work with teachers/ mentors	2	0	1
Total	11	7	7

Some interviewees in all phases felt that future CPD activities should include enough time to develop ideas effectively. Time was required to put ideas into practice, for them to have an impact, and for teachers to reflect on their work. Primary and secondary interviewees suggested longer courses. One primary headteacher explained that two-day courses would allow for a theoretical input, follow-up time to make resources, and an opportunity for teachers to evaluate the resources and share ideas and developments with others.

9.3 Nature of CPD activities

Regardless of the type of CPD activity (within school or externally provided CPD), interviewees identified the nature of the activity they would like to see in place in the future. Table 9.5 highlights their comments.

Table 9.5 Interviewee comments about the nature of future CPD activities

Future CPD activities	Primary staff	Secondary staff	Special staff
Range and variety of provision with differentiated activities to allow for different needs	4	3	2
Practical focus	2	1	5
Greater stability	1	1	1
Total	7	5	8

Nine interviewees from across the school types suggested that in future CPD activities should reflect a range of styles and variety of opportunities which would allow for different needs to be accommodated. At least two went on to suggest that the activities themselves should be differentiated in the same way that teachers are expected to differentiate activities for children.

One respondent in each type of school pleaded for stability in education, and time to consolidate the numerous initiatives and projects that had been introduced before another was introduced.

9.4 Other issues raised

Two interviewees in a primary and a special school and two in secondary schools suggested that future professional development should not be limited to education. Aromatherapy courses or exchanges with those working outside education would have a positive effect on morale and reduce stress.

Primary and special schools were more anxious about funding and the availability of supply cover than their secondary school colleagues.

In primary schools, individual aspirations for future CPD activities and their focus related to:

• valuing CPD activities and giving them status; this was not always considered to be the case at present for school-based and school-led activities

- giving teachers management opportunities before they become managers, including more opportunities to lead CPD sessions

- having a wider view of education

- being part of a coherent plan rather than *ad hoc* provision

- providing mutual support for staff.

One primary teacher felt that future CPD should provide an immediate response to her needs. The current planning required to organise CPD did not always allow for specific needs to be met. Sometimes needs or the focus changed, especially when a teacher was working with a different year group the following year.

One primary headteacher endorsed an OFSTED (OFSTED, 1997, pp. 39–40) recommendation for a directory of expertise and a record of work arranged by focus of activity. Two primary interviewees said the school needed additional space to develop CPD activities.

Secondary and special schools interviewees asked for a greater choice of activity and ownership of their own professional development. Some special school staff wanted their school to become more involved in training teachers, and others sought more stimulation by outside presenters. LSAs said that they wanted a route to progress into teaching.

9.5 Summary

- It was clear that in addition to the CPD activities that were being undertaken at present, school staff had views about what they would like to contribute to future professional development. In many cases, it was more of the kinds of activity that were already being undertaken but with appropriate time allocation. The opportunities to work with other schools when children were in school was suggested by primary interviewees. Flexibility and variety of CPD provision were called for, with teachers having a choice.

10 SUMMARY AND DISCUSSION

This chapter summarises and highlights the main findings of the research. This is followed by discussion of the issues that have emerged.

10.1 Overall summary of main findings

10.1.1 Types of CPD activities undertaken

♦ A wide range of CPD activities was undertaken by teachers, but there was no evidence of a link between length of teaching career and the type of activity undertaken.

♦ Most activities focused on teaching and learning rather than management.

♦ Similar CPD activities were identified in primary, secondary and special schools, although primary schools used demonstration lessons and observations of colleagues more frequently than their secondary and special school colleagues. Primary schools had an emphasis on literacy and numeracy; primary and secondary schools commented on ICT training, while special schools tended to develop their special educational needs expertise.

♦ The school had a leading role in determining the focus and nature of CPD activities, although support was often provided by the LEA advisers.

♦ CPD activities were offered by a range of providers: schools organised and provided many activities themselves; LEAs provided and facilitated a variety of different CPD opportunities.

♦ Very few teachers were engaged in studying abroad or using videos to enhance their professional development.

10.1.2 Processes

♦ LEAs and schools identified teachers' CPD needs in the light of national policies, and review of the EDP (by LEAs) and the SDP (by schools). Headteachers, deputy headteachers and/or the CPD coordinators from all schools reported using the SDP to identify teachers' CPD needs.

♦ Appraisal, Performance Management and self-identification (where staff recognised their own needs) were also used in the need identification processes reported by teachers.

♦ The headteacher and/or CPD coordinator played a fundamental role in teachers' CPD. They were the 'gatekeepers': first to receive external

CPD activity information (courses, conferences), which they then distributed and/or used as a basis for recommendations. They ultimately authorised staff's participation in CPD: in accordance with the aims and priorities of the SDP, and whether funding and supply cover were available.

♦ The CPD coordinator planned future CPD activities and monitored the evaluation/feedback of external CPD, attended by staff, to inform decisions on future attendance.

♦ LEAs indicated that self-report questionnaires were most frequently used to evaluate CPD activities. This information was used to inform authority-wide evaluations, or to enable course providers to revise/refocus their content.

♦ Evaluation forms were most frequently reported as being used in schools to evaluate external CPD. These recorded immediate perceptions of the CPD activity: its content, delivery, potential impact.

♦ Long-term evaluations and processes to identify the impact of CPD activities upon teaching and learning did not appear to be well established.

♦ School procedures/processes for teachers to participate in, and to evaluate, CPD were clearer for external CPD than for other forms of CPD.

10.1.3 Support strategies

Support strategies within the LEA

The LEA

♦ provided CPD activities in the form of in-school support, courses and conferences

♦ provided advisers and advisory teams who were central to the support offered

♦ collected and disseminated information about CPD opportunities

♦ fostered networks and support groups

♦ facilitated the sharing of good practice

♦ in some cases, offered funding for CPD activities

♦ developed partnerships with schools and provided central resources.

Support strategies within the school

The school provided support for teachers' CPD through:

♦ the ethos of the school

♦ the staff team, but particularly the CPD coordinator

♦ the allocation of time and funding for professional development.

10.1.4 Views of conditions that constitute effective CPD

♦ Teachers should be able to choose and direct their CPD.

♦ Personal enthusiasm and desire for professional development were seen as crucial.

♦ CPD should improve teaching skills/practice and have an effect on teaching and learning (although schools found it difficult to measure impact).

♦ Effective CPD is facilitated by a school ethos that is conductive to professional development and provides a culture of lifelong learning for all. The impetus for this tended to stem from the headteacher.

♦ CPD should have a challenging and appropriate content, meet needs at all levels (national, school, individual) and evoke ideas for practical implementation. The venue should be accessible and convenient. The delivery style should be varied and include practical demonstrations and interactive activities.

♦ The deliverer must have appropriate background knowledge and expertise.

♦ Adequate non-contact time, resources and supply cover are needed to undertake and consolidate CPD.

10.1.5 Impact of CPD upon teaching and learning

It is clear that, for CPD to be effective, it should have an impact on teaching and children's learning. However, determining a direct link between CPD and impact was difficult, as tangible evidence was not always readily available. Nevertheless, the research found that:

♦ there was an assumption/expectation that CPD will have an impact on teachers in school and in the classroom and on children's learning

♦ it was easier for teachers to identify impact on teaching than on learning

♦ CPD increased teacher confidence

♦ monitoring the impact of CPD was usually informal, although some interviewees identified more systematic procedures

♦ there was an impact on teaching and learning at both school and an individual level.

10.1.6 Improving CPD

Interviewees in the case study schools suggested:

♦ making greater use of existing activities but having time and resources to improve the conditions

♦ working with teachers in other schools, especially when children were in school

♦ flexibility and variety of CPD provision, so that teachers had more choice.

10.2 Issues arising

The two main aims of the NFER project were to identify LEA and school strategies to support the professional development of classroom teachers, and to provide detailed examples of innovative practice that might usefully be adopted by schools and LEAs wishing to improve current provision. The project examined current processes and experiences of teachers' CPD and highlighted the role of the LEA where appropriate.

Since the beginning of the project, the CPD strategy has been launched and it is interesting to note that some of the elements of the strategy were already in place in the case study schools. In particular, the notion of sharing good practice, the need to identify needs at different levels and teachers' wish to exercise more control over their choices of CPD activities and the direction of CPD were widespread.

The NFER study has described the variety of CPD activities that were in place in schools, and the implications for those working at different levels in the education system are described below.

National initiatives have focused CPD activities, and the research found that a range of different approaches, activities and providers was contributing to meeting teachers' needs. In primary schools, teachers' needs focused on implementing the National Literacy and Numeracy Strategies, while ICT training was being undertaken in most schools during the course of the research. Although teachers recognised the need to implement such initiatives, they sometimes felt that it limited the amount of choice they had in selecting and participating in their own professional development.

LEA level

The CPD strategy (DfEE, 2001b) suggests that the LEA should be one of a range of providers, and indeed the NFER study found that LEAs are already playing a significant role in providing and supporting teachers' CPD activities.

The 'Good Value CPD' (DfEE, 2001a) sets out the Government's code of practice for providers. It suggests that providers should inform schools of the details of the CPD deliverer, such as their experience and expertise, and that the target audience should be clearly indicated. It also specifies that the providers should explain their delivery methods in advance, and that the materials used should be of a high standard, be differentiated and have up-to-date content. Similar conditions for CPD were identified by interviewees in the research. Both teachers and LEA staff indicated that where activities did not meet these conditions, CPD was less effective and had less impact on teaching and learning.

The research highlights the key contributions made by LEAs in terms of:

♦ providing and facilitating CPD activities

♦ supporting schools through the work of the adviser and advisory teams

♦ fostering networks and support groups

♦ providing information about CPD opportunities both within the LEA and further afield.

In addition to facilitating CPD for meeting national priorities, the research showed that LEAs should also have systems in place which allow for the schools' SDPs to inform the LEA EDP in the same way as schools predominantly used their SDP to prioritise and direct their training needs. Where such interaction between the EDP and SDPs existed, schools were more likely to use the LEA CPD activities. It was noted that sometimes LEA priorities did not always fit with the SDP, and LEA priorities changed before schools had time to consolidate developments in school.

It was also important that clear, detailed and accurate information was provided to schools so that they could choose CPD which enabled them to meet the SDP targets and use the CPD budget effectively. Schools sought new, challenging and up-to-date ideas that could be implemented in the classroom, provided by competent and experienced trainers and experts in their field.

Furthermore, LEA-provided CPD was perceived as most appropriate when it met the needs of the school. This was most likely when the LEA staff were in touch with, and receptive to, the school's needs and context and when there was coordination between the LEA advisory team and the CPD coordinator/headteacher.

The relationships between LEA personnel and schools influenced the perception of teachers. Where advisers were well known and respected, schools benefited from the expertise. There were concerns that where LEA funding had been decreased and there was a smaller advisory team in place, schools no longer had the level of support to which they had been accustomed.

School level

At school level, headteachers were committed to developing opportunities for CPD, In many schools, there was an expectation that teachers participated in CPD, and activities were considered more effective when there was a supportive ethos and culture of professional development in the school.

CPD coordinators were key players in organising and managing CPD and, in most cases, the linchpin for individual teachers' professional development. They bridged the gap between individual and school SDP requirements. They were often the contact point for the LEA, with CPD coordinators' meetings providing a useful opportunity to plan and to disseminate information about forthcoming CPD activities.

Furthermore, they monitored staff feedback via formal/informal dissemination and evaluation forms. However, long-term monitoring and evaluation processes did not appear to have been established. It would be appropriate for the LEA adviser to feed into this school-level evaluation process, to evaluate the effectiveness of LEA- provided CPD and its impact in school. This process would also facilitate the provision of the most appropriate CPD.

Funding often controlled both the range of CPD provision and teacher participation, but perhaps the greatest challenge for teachers was time for activities. Where time was limited, it seemed that the impact of the activity was also limited: when there was no time for teachers to consolidate, follow up or reflect on ideas, they were less likely to incorporate new ideas into their teaching.

Teacher shortages have reduced the availability of supply teachers, which in turn, has restricted teachers' opportunities to undertake CPD. However, a school's reputation for providing good CPD opportunities could facilitate its recruitment and retention. On the other hand, the research found that the enhanced professional expertise acquired by teachers could lead to their promotion, but not necessarily in the same school.

Individual level

At an individual level, tensions sometimes existed between personal requirements and school demands. Teachers were undertaking CPD to ensure that they were meeting professional requirements for national priorities and to meet SDP requirements, sometimes at the expense of having a choice about developing their own particular interest and expertise. Most teachers interviewed participated fully in a range of CPD activities and were appreciative of the skills developed and expertise gained.

Impact of CPD activities

The term 'effective' is value laden. What would be reported as 'effective' in one school might be perceived differently in another school. Effective CPD was often said to be that which had an impact on teaching and learning. The research found that providing tangible evidence of impact was not always straightforward, although it was easier to evaluate how it had affected teaching than to assess the impact on children's learning.

The benefits identified by teachers arising from participation in CPD activities included increased confidence. This led them to be more aware of their own practice and willing to look for ways of implementing changes and taking on board new ideas.

The impact on children's learning was said to be reflected in improved achievement levels, a more enthusiastic approach to learning, increased self-esteem and greater collaboration. For many teachers, the impact on their teaching and children's learning was only monitored informally. Any long-term impact on changes in teaching philosophy or children's thinking and attitudes towards their learning was not identified, monitored or evaluated, although teachers were usually active in disseminating their CPD experiences to colleagues within the school.

There is clearly a need for LEAs and schools to develop LEA- and school-level systems for evaluating the short- and long-term impact of CPD activities in order to ensure that they make a significant contribution to raising standards of teaching and learning.

REFERENCES

DEPARTMENT FOR EDUCATION AND EMPLOYMENT (1998). *Teachers: Meeting the Challenge of Change* (Cm. 4164). London: The Stationery Office.

DEPARTMENT FOR EDUCATION AND EMPLOYMENT (2001a). *Good Value CPD: a Code of Practice for Providers of Professional Development for Teachers* (DfEE 0059/2001). London: DfEE.

DEPARTMENT FOR EDUCATION AND EMPLOYMENT (2001b). *Learning and Teaching: a Strategy for Professional Development*. London: DfEE.

DEPARTMENT FOR EDUCATION AND EMPLOYMENT (2001c). *Schools: Building on Success* (Cm. 5050). London: The Stationery Office.

DERRINGTON, C. (2000). *The LEA Contribution to School Improvement: a Role Worth Fighting For* (LGA Research Report 9). Slough: NFER.

FLECKNOE, M. (2000). 'Can continuing professional development for teachers be shown to raise pupils' achievement?' *Journal of In-service Education*, **26**, 3, 437–57.

HARLAND, J., ASHWORTH, M., ATKINSON, M., HALSEY, K., HAYNES, J., MOOR, H. and WILKIN, A. (1999). *Thank You for the Days? How Schools Use their Non-contact Days*. Slough: NFER.

KEATING, I. (2001). 'The efficacy of CPD: its impact upon classroom practice', *Professional Development Today*, **4**, 2, 73–8.

LEE, B. (2000). *Continuing Professional Development: Teachers' Perspectives* (Research Summary). Slough: NFER.

MORI (1995). *Survey of Continuing Professional Development: Research Study Conducted for Teacher Training Agency*. London: TTA.

OFFICE FOR STANDARDS IN EDUCATION (1997). *The Annual Report of Her Majesty's Chief Inspector of Schools: Standards and Quality in Education 1995/96*. London: The Stationery Office

APPENDICES

Appendix A.1   Advisory Body details

Ms Zoë Ollerenshaw
Local Government Association
Local Government House
Smith Square
London
SW1P 3HZ

Mr Ian Terrell
Chair of the International Professional Development Association
Head of CPD Anglia Polytechnic University
School of Education
Rivermead Campus
Bishop Hall Lane
Chelmsford
Essex CM1 1SQ

Ms Gussie Anderson
Headteacher
Wormholt Park Primary School
Bryony Road
London
W12 0SR

Mr Jacques Szemalikowski
Deputy Headteacher
Grey Court School
Ham Street
Ham
TW10 7HN

Dr P Elfed-Owens
LEA Adviser
Education Department
Government Building
Dinerch Road
Colwyn Bay
LL28 4UL

Dr John Harland
Head of NFER Northern Office
Genesis 4
York Science Park
University Road
Heslington
York
YO10 5DG

Appendix A2.1
Interviewees within primary schools: roles/responsibilities and experience

Primary School	Roles/responsibilities	Experience in years	
		At this school	Total
1	Headteacher	15	18
	Acting deputy headteacher/ subject coordinator/mentor for NQTs	5	8
	CPD coordinator/subject coordinator	3.5	not given
2	Headteacher	4	27
	CPD coordinator/deputy headteacher/ subject coordinator	25	25
	Subject coordinator	26	27
	Subject coordinator	10	28
3	Headteacher/SENCO	3	12
	Deputy headteacher/ Staff Development Officer	23	23
	SENCO/subject coordinator	4	6
	Subject coordinator	8	9
4	Headteacher/CPD coordinator	5	28
	Deputy headteacher/ subject coordinator	12	18
	Subject coordinator	12	12
	Subject coordinator	3	4
5	Headteacher/CPD coordinator	8	22
	Subject coordinator	29	32
	Teacher	2	4
	Secretary/administrator	6	6
6	Headteacher	5	20
	Deputy headteacher/ subject coordinator	26	26
	CPD coordinator/IIP coordinator	25	31
	Mentor/subject coordinator	18	20
	Mentor/subject coordinator	6	8
7	Headteacher	25	28
	Deputy headteacher/ subject coordinator/INSET coordinator	12	22
	Subject coordinator/NOF trainer	23	30
	Subject coordinator	2	7

Appendix A2.1 (*continued*)

Primary School	Roles/responsibilities	Experience in years	
		At this school	Total
8	Headteacher	3.5	30
	Deputy headteacher/CPD coordinator/ subject coordinator	2	28
	Subject coordinator	5.5	6
	Subject coordinator	7	7
9	Headteacher	10	20
	CPD coordinator/subject coordinator	2	10
	SENCO	2.5	10
	Learning Support Staff	3	10
10	Head Teacher/CPD coordinator team	9	22
	Acting deputy headteacher/ subject coordinator	3	7
	Subject coordinator	2	3
11	Headteacher	3	not given
	Subject coordinator	3	3
	Subject coordinator	2	10
12	Headteacher	not given	17
	SENCO/subject coordinator	2	7
	Deputy headteacher/CPD coordinator	not given	18
	Subject coordinator	2	2

Appendix A2.2
Interviewees within secondary schools: roles/responsibilities and experience

Secondary School	Roles/responsibilities	Experience in years	
		At this school	Total
1	Headteacher	8	32
	Head of department	2	8
	Head of department	23	23
	Teacher	12	10
	Assistant head of department	10	10
2	Headteacher	6	27
	Head of department	24	21
	Business link coordinator	25	25
	CPD coordinator/deputy headteacher	9	23
	Subject coordinator	6	7
3	Headteacher	14	35
	CPD coordinator	not given	17
	Teacher	6	14
	Teacher	6	28
	Teacher	not given	24
	Teacher/mentor	19	31

Appendix A2.3
Interviewees within special schools: roles/responsibilities and experience

Special School	Roles/responsibilities	Experience in years	
		At this school	Total
1	Headteacher	18	33
	Deputy headteacher	18	24
	Deputy headteacher/subject coordinator	18	18
	Deputy of unit	27	27
	Subject coordinator	10	10
	Nursery nurse	5	8
	Nursery nurse	22	12
2	Headteacher	13	29
	Deputy headteacher	12	23
	Special needs support assistant	10	10
	Special needs support assistant	13	13
	Teacher	3	3
3	Headteacher	not given	24
	Deputy headteacher/CPD coordinator	6	25
	Subject coordinator	6	6
	Subject coordinator	21	21
	Special support assistant (f/t)	6	6
	Special support assistant (f/t)	14	14

Appendix A4.1
School staff undertaking CPD other than at school

Role	No. of years teaching	No. of years in post	CPD activities
Primary school staff			
Headteacher	30	5	LSPH, PIPS, SFA EXCEL training, HT +coordinator networks Literacy/numeracy training
SENCO History, PE, RE coordinator	6	5.5	SFA, PSHE scheme Cluster group meetings
KS 1 manager, Science/IT coordinator	3	2	MA LEA middle management training NOF trainer LEA update on curriculum areas
SENCO KS1 coordinator	7	2	LEA – Early Years initiate SEN courses
SENCO/PE/ discipline responsibility	6	4	SENCO courses/conferences DASE
Maths coordinator	10	2	LEA coordinator support courses/ conferences Learning to Learn project
NNEB	8	5	BA Hons to graduate teacher programme
School administrator	6	3	ATT
Secondary school staff			
Headteacher	34	14	SMT courses and involvement in management training
Science teacher	14	6	CASE
HOD English	23	9	LEA, HOD meetings/groups LEA, HEI courses IQEA
Special school staff			
Acting Deputy PE and RE coordinator	7	3	MA
Deputy of the Autistic Unit	27	Not given	Autistic society LEA courses for SEN

Appendix A4.2
Staff undertaking only school-focused and school based CPD activities

Role	No. of years teaching	No. of years in post	CPD activities
Primary school staff			
Headteacher	20	5	School focused as part of a project outside the school
Year 2 teacher RE coordinator	10	8	Policy writing. When she took over there was nothing in place. Reflection on children's learning
CPD coordinator	30	2	ICT NOF IiP which were school focused. Also been involved in leading training within the school
Deputy	18	12	Already does a lot in school, e.g. demonstration lessons, leading INSET, staff meetings and steps into other coordinators shoes when required
KS 1, PSHE and PE coordinator	7	2	Been using OFSTED model of school self-evaluation and is heavily engaged in monitoring and observing in school
Special school staff			
SNSA	10	10	Focus on training in school relating to SEN

Appendix A4.3
Interviewees involved in accredited study

Role	No. of years teaching	No. of years in post	Course of study
Primary school staff			
Headteacher	27	4	MA
SENCO/language language	4	2	DASE
Headteacher	22	6	MSc
SENCO	10	2.5	MEd
Headteacher	12	3	DASE leading to a Master's degree
SENCO	6	4	DASE
Deputy/CPD coordinator	20	4	Master's degree
KS 1 coordinator	3	2	MA tailor made to fit middle management interests
Headteacher	22	4	MA
Deputy	7	3	MA
Secondary school staff			
CPD coordinator	23	9	MBA, NVQ level 5
Special school staff			
Deputy	24	12	MSc
Headteacher	33	18	MSc
Headteacher	29	13	Diploma in SEN
Deputy	20	1	Diploma in SEN
KS2, PE, IT and PSHE coordinator	21	6	MA
Deputy	20	3	MEd
Year 2 and ICT coordinator	10	10	MEd
NNEB	8	5	BA
SNSA	13	13	OU degree

Appendix A4.4
Special projects

IQEA

IQEA was a project run by an HEI. It focused on the classroom and encouraged teachers to try out new teaching methods. It encouraged a self-sufficient school and generated new ideas. One secondary school and one primary school in the case study schools were taking part in the IQEA. In the primary school involved in IQEA, the headteacher was

enthusiastic about the work. The teachers talked about how it was affecting them in the classroom. Involvement in the project started with the headteacher being inspired at a conference. She then persuaded the HEI to get involved in a primary focus where previously it had concentrated on secondary schools. She talked with the team at the HEI and persuaded her local secondary school and another primary school in their cluster to get involved.

As part of the project she had been involved in:
- an audit of provision in school
- a trial of activities in the classroom
- work with other schools
- an international conference for training and reflection
- the dissemination of ideas throughout the school.

In the secondary school, the headteacher commented that he had

attended a training session and the school now had 18 out of the 62 teachers involved in the project. He considered that the project set an impetus for the school, gave continuity across subject areas. There were training sessions with ideas presented being implemented into teaching. Teachers were encouraged to cascade to others, to evaluate and discuss their work at regular intervals.

One secondary school teacher interviewed identified that involvement in the project had given him the opportunity to:

- lead INSET

- model lessons to staff

- do classroom observations

- visit schools nationally to talk about the project

- take part in an international visit to set up the project abroad.

Other teachers in the school and involved in IQEA commented that they had follow- up courses, timetabled weekly meetings that had an agenda but allowed for open discussion about issues arising, and delivered presentations about their work within the school and in other schools.

None of the special schools in the case studies was involved in IQEA.

Investors in People (IiP)

In the schools where Investors In People (IiP) was a special project, it led to the view that training should include the whole staff team. In primary schools, this extended to the caretaker completing a Duke of Edinburgh Award, a lunchtime supervisor undertaking training in dealing with pupil behaviour, a school secretary undertaking accountancy qualifications and a learning support assistant attending Welsh evening classes.

New Opportunities Fund (NOF)

NOF training for ICT was mentioned as being part of professional development by seven teachers or headteachers in six primary schools and by three teachers in two secondary schools. It may well be that other teachers were also involved in NOF training but it was not what they saw as the main focus for their professional development.

In the primary schools, the teachers who commented on NOF training were in fact themselves trainers. They had attended training and were now sharing their expertise with others. One interviewee explained how:

she had been involved in selecting the provider after several had been invited into school to do a presentation. They chose the one that was able to meet the different needs of the staff and offered flexibility in study time and group support. They offered a basic skills unit and the curriculum support materials were appropriate.

Frustrations were voiced about children knowing more about ICT than the teachers and the training had '*broadened horizons and gained confidence*' but as yet not all staff were online.

In one secondary school, the CPD coordinator identified 38 members of staff being involved in NOF training. Some had undertaken the training and were now sharing their expertise with the rest of the staff. It was usually arranged for two hours per week after school.

There were criticisms from participants in secondary schools about the quality of the guidelines and lack of differentiation for participants with different levels of skill. However, one teacher felt that the curriculum content was good although it was frustrating when systems failed. Another teacher felt that she now used IT more but the materials did not meet her needs. She had increased confidence but felt that the training was too theoretical as she already had typing and keyboard skills.

No one in the special schools visited in this research mentioned NOF training.

Success For All (SFA)

A project identified by one primary school was similar to IQEA in that it involved working with an HEI on a school-focused issue. The Success for All (SFA) project originated in the USA from the Reading Recovery programme after adaptations in response to research. The philosophy is based on children working in teams so that they are involved in thinking and discussion. Management signals are taught to children and used by teachers to act as cues for children's behaviour response.

As the headteacher involved explained,

All the children were tested to establish their reading age, then grouped according to ability. The narrow ability range helped teachers with their planning. The SFA programme was used for one-and-a-half hours each day. It was a structured and prescriptive programme with specific resources, on loan from the university and directed at children's reading age. It broadly followed the National Literacy Strategy, which she thought was becoming more like SFA. The programme was developed in this school in response to a poor level of reading. The university staff visited the school, the headteacher visited other schools that were using the programme and the university gave a presentation to the staff, who then voted on implementing it in school. The vote was positive, and they were now half-way through a three-year pilot.

Three members of staff in this school are SFA trainers and involvement in the programme has given them opportunities to:

- work with class teachers within the school to help them deliver lessons and refine teaching styles. This resulted in observing lessons, discussing performance and writing reports to identify future development in the classroom

- visit the USA for conferences and school visits

- offer training in other schools locally, nationally and in Educational Action Zones.

Learning to Learn

This project also involved working with an HEI. In this case, the focus was on child development and learning styles. It was linked to developing children's thinking skills and recognising multiple intelligences. The school was one of five working together on the project. It had enabled staff to:

- work with university staff

- reflect on current practice.

In this school, teachers had been encouraged to

think differently about their teaching and to be aware of different teaching styles. The CPD activity was led by a consultant who contributed to a twilight session. The school was also supplied with documents to enable teachers to follow up ideas at a later date. Another teacher involved in the project felt that it was like being back at university and was really making them think about children's thinking. He recognised that it was not only having an effect in his classroom now, but that a much larger impact would be felt in the future with his change of attitude towards teaching and learning.

PHSE

In one primary school, teachers were involved in a PSHE scheme. It had been set up in Canada and introduced children to the idea of adult responsibilities. Three schools in the LEA were involved and the link with the secondary school had initiated the involvement in the project. It was a two-term programme guided by a booklet of lessons. Representatives from the programme were evaluating it; they observed in school and talked with teachers about the suitability for the local area.

Nurture groups

CPD activities relating to establishing nurture groups was identified as influential in one primary school where two of the four interviewed talked about their involvement in a four-day training course at an HEI where attention was given to theoretical and practical elements of nurture groups. The school had been looking for a way of responding to a group of children whose behaviour was becoming a cause for concern. Two members of staff attended the course, implemented ideas in school and then shared their experiences with other schools within the LEA as well as advisers and teachers visiting the school to see the programme in action.

Other projects

First Steps was identified as a special project in one primary school. It was provided, and supported financially, by the LEA but no further details were given. Another school mentioned involvement in Aiming and Healthy School. No further details were provided.

In the secondary schools, interviewees identified their involvement in achieving Beacon status, being a learning mentor and having links with industry as contributing to their professional development.

Beacon status

For one science teacher, the pursuit of Beacon status for the school had provided the opportunity to work with other teachers in other comprehensive schools where demonstration lessons were provided. The funding for applying for Beacon status allowed time to be available to develop ways of working together to the benefit of all the schools involved.

Learning mentor training

One head of year and maths teacher with a learning mentor role had been involved in specific training for that role. She had hoped to be involved in five days' national training at her local teachers' centre. She attended for two of the days but felt that it did not really meet her needs and she was unable to attend the other sessions because of lack of supply cover.

Links with industry

Education Business Partnership (EBD) had been part of one secondary teacher's professional development in the past. The focus had changed and the school was no longer involved. It had enabled pupils to visit different employment opportunities to see where a career in science could lead. For example, they visited a hospital pathology laboratory and Marconi. She went on to add that even though she welcomed the opportunities, sometimes the representative of the organisation was not able to communicate effectively with schoolchildren.

Special school staff used CPD opportunities to focus on specific educational needs reflecting the demands made by the children with whom they worked.

EDY and TEACCH

EDY and TEACCH were used with children with autism. They are structured approaches with strong links to an HEI. There is a structured timetable and use was made of photographs and words. It helped to control behaviour. In one school, a combination of these two approaches was used for working with children with varying degrees of autism.

PIPs

Progress in Phonics (PIPs) was run by the LEA at a family centre. The deputy headteacher who had attended was impressed, and used it herself in the classroom before introducing it to and adopting it throughout the school.

TOPS

TOPS was identified by a teacher in a special school who commented that it was provided by the LEA and hosted at a local primary school. The day courses were practical and involved discussion. He had also attended other similar courses and mentioned Healthy School, standard gymnastics and sport development.

Communication development programme

This CPD activity included a course for teachers and support staff to learn to use Makaton and BSL so that they were able to provide an interactive curriculum where appropriate. Sometimes these specialist courses were also available for parents and other school staff. One school developed a project centred on the need for children to communicate with each other.

As the teacher involved in managing and organising it explained,

It was part of a whole package that emerged from SDP plan. Subject coordinators identified the need to develop children's communication skills. As a result, a communication coordinator's role was created and communication groups within the humanities were started. Children were grouped by taking into account their level of ability to communicate. This meant that the children who were not confident machine users were given opportunities to develop those skills so that they were able to take part in later lessons more confidently. Teachers realised that being unable to communicate either through their machines or through Signing was holding children back. So they wanted to develop a Signing culture in school which enabled all children and staff to communicate with each other even if they did not have access to their communication machines.

The idea came from the speech therapist, the hearing impaired adviser and the communication coordinator. They involved a teacher for a twilight session which then developed into something more permanent with several teachers gaining a certificate in BSL.

The adviser and speech therapist supported the coordinator and school with another day's training. Not all teachers felt confident in using this different grouping method, so videos were made to share practice and expertise. They also had time when other schools came in to see what they had achieved. The headteacher commented that children's levels of achievement had gone up tremendously. It was the lack of confidence in using their communication machines that was holding them back rather than anything else.

Subject-oriented projects

Some schools were involved in subject-focused projects.

Literacy and numeracy CPD activities were found in all the case study primary schools. They were usually led by the LEA adviser and supported by the school language coordinator. One example is described below.

For one literacy coordinator who was new to the post, the National Literacy Strategy provided her with an opportunity to look at practice in the school, attend the LEA training sessions for language coordinators and give feedback ideas to staff in twilight sessions. The LEA had instigated the activity in response to Government initiatives. The course was considered to be effective because:

- it was new and challenging

- it allowed her time to plan the feedback to staff and the implementation in school

- she met up with other language coordinators

- it enabled professional partnerships to be developed between schools

- it provided the opportunity for reappraisal at the literacy provision within the school

- it involved working with the LEA adviser in school, which developed confidence

- it generated new systems for monitoring provision and to identify further requirements.

In one secondary school Cognitive Acceleration in Science Education (CASE) was identified as science-based activity. It was used by most schools in the LEA and involved

one-day training with an external trainer from CASE followed by work with the Science department on one of the designated curriculum development closure days. The course provider brought in all the resources and equipment needed for the first ten lessons, and talked through the principles, theory, practicalities and organisation with the teachers as well as giving them the opportunity to undertake the experiments as the children would be asked to do. This enabled the teachers to identify the challenges and pitfalls of undertaking the activities with children. Subsequent twilight sessions were used to look at other materials and lessons.

One teacher accompanied the head of department to observe a CASE lesson in the LEA. They were able to develop paired observation and feedback skills.

A4.5   Further professional study

Interviewees were studying for higher degrees and a few other courses.

Higher degrees

Staff involved in accredited higher study commented on how they were able to focus their area of study to accommodate their own interests, and use the ideas within the school. Most Master's degrees allowed students to select relevant modules. Self-study modules were also used. Teachers were able to develop an area of expertise in greater depth.

For two primary schools and one secondary school, the 'partnership' they had with the HEI was important. It provided an opportunity for teachers to gain credit towards a Master's degree through the induction training they carried out in order to mentor students undertaking the school experience component of their initial teacher training. In another school, the headteacher commented on the preferential treatment they received from the HEI for having student teachers in the school for their school experiences. Further details were not provided.

Partnerships between the HEI, LEA and the school were mentioned in schools where there was joint funding from the LEA and HEI. In a few cases, school staff had become involved in higher education and had been asked to contribute to courses run by the HEI. Teachers' involvement ranged from a secondment for a year to delivering a subject knowledge-based lecture to students completing a PGCE. One primary headteacher undertaking an education management masters degree explained:

> *I have used the opportunity to focus ideas for my own school but*
> *I have been able to visit other schools similar to my own but who*
> *are achieving more. I have observed teaching, looked at resources,*
> *buildings and gathered ideas for my own SDP.*

In this school, there was a strong commitment to accredited study. All the interviewees in the school were at various stages of a Master's programme. This gave the staff a global view of education and when more than one person was engaged in study, they felt able to support each other. Where this was happening in another school, the HEI delivered the modules in school.

Other courses

A few interviewees were involved in study towards a degree or diploma. The two studying for a degree were using it to develop their career prospects from being a learning support assistant to becoming a teacher. Two other LSAs commented that they were undertaking a course specifically for LSAs but were unsure what opportunities were available for them upon completion of the course.

The Diploma in Advanced Studies in Education (DASE) enabled teachers to gain qualifications at different stages leading up to a Master's degree. It was supported by the LEA/HEI partnership and encouraged students to look at both theoretical and practical issues. The needs of the individual could be catered for, and in one special school it enabled a teacher to move towards teaching pupils with specific rather than general learning difficulties.